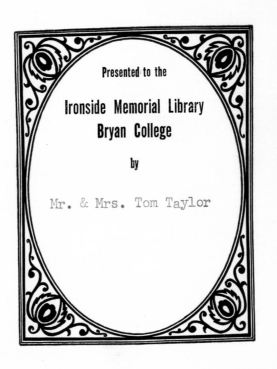

THE FRENCH REVOLUTION

THE FRENCH REVOLUTION

ALBERT GOODWIN

REVISED EDITION

HARPER TORCHBOOKS
THE ACADEMY LIBRARY
HARPER & ROW, PUBLISHERS
NEW YORK

THE FRENCH REVOLUTION

This book was originally published in the History series of the Hutchinson University Library in 1953, with second, third, and fourth revised editions in 1956, 1965, and 1966, respectively. It is here reprinted by arrangement with Hutchinson & Co., Ltd., London.

First HARPER TORCHBOOK edition published 1962 by Harper & Row, Publishers, Incorporated 49 East 33rd Street, New York, N.Y. 10016.

CONTENTS

I

THE 'ANCIEN REGIME'

(i) *Introduction*

The immediate causes of the French revolution of 1789 must be sought, not in the economic grievances of the peasants, nor in the political discontents of the middle class, but in the reactionary aspirations of the French aristocracy. Though the revolution established the political power and consolidated the economic position of the middle class, it was set in motion by the aristocracy in the years 1787 and 1788 in the attempt to defend its own fiscal and and political privileges, which were threatened by the reforming policy of the Bourbon monarchy. The decision of Louis XVI, in July 1788, to summon the States General, or national representative assembly, which had not met since 1614, marked the Crown's capitulation to the concerted pressure of the lay, ecclesiastical, and judicial aristocracy. These privileged classes expected that the adoption of the traditional method of voting in the States General—by order and not by head—would enable them, not only to prevent radical reform, but also to consolidate their victory over the Crown by a similar subjugation of the third estate. This gross miscalculation rendered inevitable a revolution which might well have been avoided by the nobility's acceptance of the consequences of political and fiscal equality.

The political crisis of 1787–8 revealed clearly to a hitherto unorganised middle class the need to defend its interests against aristocratic reaction and stimulated its political consciousness by associating it in the work of national regeneration. When the States General met at Versailles in May 1789 the third estate, consisting

almost entirely of middle-class representatives, was thus ready and
determined to challenge the temporary ascendancy of the privileged
orders and to take over and put into operation many of the plans
elaborated by the reforming ministers of the *ancien régime*. By
defending its own rights and those of the French nation against the
nobility, and by asserting the sovereignty and legislative initiative
of the National Assembly against the Crown, the middle class
won a control over the revolution, which was never seriously
compromised by the independent action of the peasants or urban
proletariat.

Before the governmental crisis of 1787–8 can be explained, however, it is necessary to describe briefly the financial embarrassments,
the administrative confusion and the agrarian distress which characterised the declining years of the *ancien régime*.

(ii) *Faulty finance*

The chief weakness of France's pre-revolutionary form of government was faulty finance. Throughout the eighteenth century, there
had existed a serious annual deficit. This legacy of the wars of Louis
XIV had been perpetuated by increasing governmental expenditure
and by the inelasticity of the state revenue. To some extent, the
increase in the cost of administration reflected a steady rise in general
prices since 1733, greater expenditure on public works, notably on
road improvements, and an increasing tendency of the central
government to take over, from local or ecclesiastical authorities,
some of the responsibility for public assistance, poor relief and
medical care. The recurring French deficits of the eighteenth century,
however, may be attributed predominantly to the cost of the country's
wars. Between 1733 and 1783 France waged four wars, the total
cost of which has been estimated at approximately 4,000,000,000
livres or about £200,000,000. The Seven Years' War (1756–63) had
been a world-wide contest for colonial and maritime supremacy in
which France, besides maintaining her own forces, had been called
upon to subsidise heavily those of her new ally and former hereditary
rival, Austria. France's participation in the War of American
Independence, although confined, for the most part, to naval and
financial assistance, had even more disastrous consequences. Turgot's
warning to the young Louis XVI in August 1774 that 'the first gun-
shot would drive the state into bankruptcy' was, in substance,
fulfilled. The actual expenditure on the war, variously computed at
between 1,800,000,000 and 2,000,000,000 *livres*, represented, in itself,

a severe drain on French finance. The problem of dealing with the inevitably rising deficit was further complicated by the way in which the war had been financed. Jacques Necker, who had been in charge of the finances from October 1776 to May 1781, was a Swiss banker with exaggerated, and partly erroneous, notions of the power of credit. He had, accordingly, made a point of financing the war entirely by borrowing. He had defended this policy by the plausible, but specious argument that the limit of taxable capacity had already been exceeded, and by contending that an increasing population and rising general prices would prevent an inflated public debt from being a serious burden on the financial strength of the country, even in the absence of a sinking fund for its regular repayment. To float his successive loans, Necker had been compelled to offer rates of interest varying from $8\frac{1}{2}$ to 10 per cent, and had also misrepresented the state of French finances. Hitherto, in France, public finance had been a jealously guarded state secret but, in February 1781, in order to attract investors, Necker had published his celebrated *Compte Rendu au Roi sur les finances de la Nation*, in which he announced a surplus of revenue over expenditure amounting to 10,000,000 *livres*. In fact, the deficit, at that period, was well over 46,000,000 *livres*. Unfortunately, although this report was received in ministerial circles with the scepticism it deserved, its misleading figures were accepted by the uninformed general public, which had no means of checking its calculations. The full seriousness of France's situation after the War of American Independence was thus never realised and Necker had placed almost insuperable obstacles in the way of effective post-war financial retrenchment.

The extent to which French finance had been disrupted by war may be judged from the fact that in 1788, at a time when the total state expenditure amounted to just under 630,000,000 *livres*, the interest charge on the public debt alone stood at 318,000,000 *livres*. The estimated expenditure on the defence and diplomatic services for the same year came to 165,500,000. Thus, at the end of the *ancien régime*, over three-quarters of the annual state expenditure was being incurred on defence and on the service of the public debt, itself mainly the result of previous wars. The essence of the financial problem on the eve of the revolution was, therefore, the impossibility of reducing these heavy items of national expenditure, for otherwise public credit would be dangerously undermined and national security imperilled. This meant that financial retrenchment could only be attempted in the field of civil expenditure.

The civil estimates for 1788, however, standing at 146,000,000 *livres*, represented only 23 per cent of the total expenditure. Nor would drastic economy at court have afforded any real relief, for the cost of the royal establishment and of grants to pensioners and courtiers formed under 6 per cent of the total outgoings.

Owing to the structural rigidities of the cumbrous financial system and the tenacious defence of their fiscal immunities by the privileged orders, the prospects of abolishing the deficit by expanding the revenue seemed hardly less remote. It is true that, since the middle of the century, the indirect taxes on consumers' goods—the infamous and inequitable salt tax (*gabelle*), the obsolete internal customs duties (*traites*), and the miscellaneous excise duties (*aides*) had been yielding an increasing revenue, owing to the rise in prices, an increase in the urban population and heightened rates of duty. But the benefit of the increased receipts from this source went, not into the treasury, but into the pockets of the farmers-general. These were a group of powerful financiers to whom the indirect taxes were leased out in return for a fixed money payment, which could only be increased by the treasury once every six years, as the contract fell in for renewal.

Similarly, the yield from the direct taxes could only have been permanently increased by a radical reform of the machinery of collection and by the destruction of the fiscal exemptions of the clergy, the lay nobility and a host of middle-class office-holders. Indeed, the whole tendency in the eighteenth century was for the revenue from this source to shrink rather than to expand, since the monarchy continued to sell offices carrying exemption from direct taxation. It is not true to say that the nobility was entirely exempt from direct taxes, for the lay aristocracy had, since 1695, been liable to the poll tax (*capitation*) and, since 1749, to the twentieths (*ving-tièmes*). Although the clergy had redeemed its liability to the poll tax at the beginning of the eighteenth century, it regularly voted to the Crown benevolences (*dons gratuits*) in lieu of the twentieths, whilst the clergy of certain frontier provinces, who were not represented in the quinquennial clerical assemblies, actually paid the twentieths. Nevertheless, the nobility, the clergy, and all holders of state or municipal offices were exempt from the most important and most oppressive of the direct taxes—the *taille*. Except in the frontier provinces, where the mediaeval provincial estates had survived, this tax was an arbitrary levy on the presumed wealth of the taxpayer and fell almost exclusively on the peasants.[1] Special reductions were also made by the royal tax officials in the assessment of the nobility's liability to the poll tax. It was thus that the country's peace-time financial embarrassments were due, not only to the lack of any proper budgetary or accounting system, but also to the combination of a mediaeval social structure, based on the distinction of separate 'orders', with the absence of any uniform system of administration. Effective financial reform in eighteenth-century France would, therefore, necessarily have implied changes tantamount to social and political revolution. Privilege was so intertwined with contract, social ranks so closely associated with special favours, and the canon-law obligations of the clergy as trustees for their material endowments so binding, that the extinction of fiscal exemptions could only have been imposed by an all-powerful sovereign.

(iii) *Administrative complexity*

The power exercised by French kings in the eighteenth century, however, fell far short of absolutism. Though Louis XV could, in claiming legislative omnicompetence for the Crown, appeal as late as 1770 to the divine right theory of kingship, and though the opposition inveighed against what it called 'ministerial despotism', the authority of the Bourbon monarchy was subject to powerful political checks. Despite the work of Richelieu, Mazarin, and Louis XIV, it was hemmed in and hampered by the surviving relics of feudalism. The corporate organisation of the Gallican Church, the independent position and prestige of the *parlements* or High Courts of Appeal, and the contractual relationship between the Crown and the *pays d'états*,[2] were effective stumbling-blocks in the way of a monarchy whose credit and influence had steadily declined throughout the century. The complete bureaucratic centralisation, which Tocqueville later regarded as characteristic of the *ancien régime*, was more of a dream than a reality.

It is difficult, at this distance of time, to grasp the vast power and influence of the Gallican Church in pre-revolutionary France. This influence was derived, partly from the social precedence accorded to its members, partly from its control over education, poor relief and hospitals, and partly from its monopoly of the registration of

1. The weight of direct taxation falling on the nobility was, however, considerable, see B. Behrens, 'Nobles, Privileges and Taxes in France at the end of the Ancien Régime', *Economic History Review*, 2nd series, vol. XV (1963), pp. 451–475.

2. See p. 17

births, deaths and marriages. Its power was the consequence of its great temporal endowments, the preponderant role played by the bishops in the civil administration of the *pays d'états*, its possession of a separate fiscal and judicial system, and its retention of the privilege of holding meetings of its Clerical Assembly every five years. The church may have been discredited by the theological wrangles between the Jansenists and the Jesuits in the first half of the century and weakened later by the anti-clerical onslaught of the *philosophes*, but its power as a great corporate institution within the state remained impressive.

This corporate existence was jealously guarded by the periodical assemblies, whose primary functions were the administration of the clerical estates and the exercise of the right of self-taxation. Under the contract of Poissy, concluded in December 1561 with Charles IX, the French clergy had obtained the right of not being taxed without its consent, in return for an undertaking to pay annual contributions to defray the interest on certain loans raised by the municipality of Paris in favour of the royal treasury. Consequent upon these arrangements, there had met, from 1580 onwards, representative quinquennial assemblies of the French Church. These were of two kinds. Every ten years, the contract relating to the Paris loans was renewed by an assembly to which were summoned four deputies (two to represent the bishops, and two the lower clergy) from each of the eighteen ecclesiastical provinces which formed part of the kingdom in 1561. At regular intervals five years after the meetings of these large assemblies, smaller gatherings of the same type but with half the total membership, met to consider the accounts and financial resources of the church. From the time of Louis XIV these smaller assemblies were summoned also at irregular intervals to consider demands from the treasury for the voting of clerical subsidies or benevolences. The chief advantage of these assemblies for the clergy was that they enabled the church to resist direct taxation by the state. The self-taxing power carried with it a fiscal administration independent of the lay authority and thus made it possible, to some extent, for the clergy to conceal from the treasury their real taxable capacity. Although the clergy contributed indirectly to the state revenue, this organisation enabled them to maintain the fiction that such subventions were benevolences (*dons gratuits*) which could be made or refused at will. With the consent of the treasury, these sums were, moreover, borrowed by the church from capitalists. It was, therefore, only the interest on these loans which was levied by the church in the way of self-taxation. In this way, there gradually accumulated during the course of the eighteenth century a substantial clerical debt, secured on the ecclesiastical estates. In effect, the state was merely using the superior financial credit of the church to borrow sums, the payment of which in direct taxation would have been obstinately resisted by the clergy. This convenience to the treasury, however, was more than offset by the continuance of a mechanism, which not only bolstered up the highly privileged position of the clergy, but gave the church the means of defending itself against the repeated attempts of the monarchy to subject it to direct taxation.

Even greater powers of offering resistance to the fiscal demands of a reforming monarchy were those possessed by the French *parlements*. These high courts of justice, which were of great antiquity, were essentially courts of appeal. As such, they reviewed judgements given in the inferior courts of the bailliwicks, sénéchaussés and prévôtés, into which the country was divided for judicial purposes. At the end of the eighteenth century there were thirteen of these Sovereign Courts, as they were called, the most powerful being the *parlement* of Paris.[1] Each of these *parlements* consisted of a close corporation of rich magistrates, whose offices, acquired by purchase from the state, had become, in the course of time, hereditary. Recruited orginally from prosperous middle-class families, these magistrates had attained the status of nobility (*noblesse de robe*) and thus come to enjoy the same fiscal immunities as the rest of the lay aristocracy.

Besides their judicial functions, however, the *parlements* claimed and exercised certain political powers. These were derived from the right of registering royal edicts and ordinances, possessed since the beginning of the fourteenth century by the *parlement* of Paris. From the beginning of the fifteenth century this court had begun to arrogate to itself the right of verifying and remonstrating against royal legislation, the form or substance of which it considered inconsistent with previous legislation or at variance with certain 'fundamental laws' of the monarchy. The framing of such 'remonstrances' had the effect of deferring the registration of royal edicts and preventing the recognition of their full legality until such time as the king either

1. Paris (1302), Toulouse (1443), Grenoble (1453), Bordeaux (1472), Dijon (1477), Rouen (1515), Aix-en-Provence (1501), Rennes (1554), Pau (1620), Metz (1633), Besançon (1676), Douai (1700), Nancy (1776). Eleven out of these thirteen towns still possess Appeal Courts.

revised them in accordance with the *parlement*'s wishes, or overcame the resistance to them by means of an enforced registration (*lit de justice*). Although it is difficult to compare such rights with the judicial review later exercised by the American Supreme Court, they did endow the *parlements* with the power of checking and thwarting the theoretically absolute monarchy. This was particularly true in the field of finance, for the *parlements* now claimed to exercise the power of consent to taxation formerly possessed by the States General.

Although the Bourbon monarch still asserted his legislative omni-competence, although he could, in the last resort, enforce his will on the *parlements* by means of a *lit de justice*, or by 'exiling' the magistrates to small provincial towns until they repented, the decline in the authority and prestige of the Crown in the eighteenth century made it increasingly difficult to repress this political opposition. Fundamentally, this was because the *parlements* were, until the political crisis of 1788, in a better tactical position than the monarchy to appeal to progressive public opinion. They were able to represent Louis XV's frequent recourse to *lits de justice* as an arbitrary misuse of the royal prerogative; they were able to incite a popular campaign against the royal use of *lettres de cachet* as a dangerous threat to the liberty of the subject;[1] they were able to accredit the view that royal attempts to break down fiscal privileges were, in reality, only the exactions of an oppressive and inefficient treasury. By their resistance, the *parlements* forced the monarchy to make exaggerated pretensions to political sovereignty, which it was then easy for them to depict as the sign and symbol of encroaching monarchical despotism. Against such authoritarian claims the *parlements* appealed to the vague but significant concept of fundamental laws, to contractual theories of the state and even to the idea of popular sovereignty. Historians, indeed, are now inclining towards the view that the *parlements* did even more to promote liberal political theories in eighteenth-century France than the *philosophes*.

In the field of fiscal administration, the *parlements* had discredited the currency manipulations of John Law at the time of the Regency and they had restricted the scope of Machault's efforts to secure greater fiscal equality after the Austrian Succession War. Similarly, they had been mainly responsible for the defeat of the Physiocratic reform schemes of Turgot in 1776 and for the overthrow of Necker

1. These were letters signed by the king, countersigned by one of his ministers and closed with the royal seal (*cachet*). By this means the sovereign could sentence a subject to imprisonment without trial or opportunity of defence.

in 1781.[1] As defenders of the constitutional liberties of the Gallican
Church they had, throughout the first half of the century, sided with
the Jansenists against the Jesuits, and in 1764 had brought about the
destruction in France of the Society of Jesus. It was an impressive
record of opposition which had been made possible by the solidarity
of the provincial *parlements* with the *parlement* of Paris, the calling
of sympathetic judicial strikes in support of each other, and by their
alliance with the provincial estates against the centralising policy of
the royal *intendants* and provincial governors.[2] A power which could
thus arrest the progress of financial and social reform, bring royal
justice, at least temporarily, to a complete stop and, on occasions,
throw provincial administration into confusion, was one which
could be curbed only by a strong king like Louis XIV or destroyed
by an enlightened despot. This had been eventually recognised by
Louis XV, who had supported his Chancellor Maupeou in 1771
in striking down the political powers of the *parlements* by abolishing
the Parisian court outright and by endowing a new system of appeal
courts with functions narrowly restricted to the judicial sphere.
Unfortunately, this act, which might have been the salvation of the
French monarchy, had been reversed in 1774 by the youthful and
inexperienced Louis XVI, on the advice of Maurepas. The *parlements* were thus restored to a position where they could continue to
harass royal ministers and circumvent financial reform, whilst
posing as the champions of popular rights and liberties.

Among the surviving relics of feudalism in eighteenth-century
France must also be reckoned the provincial estates, or local representative assemblies, which still continued to meet periodically in
certain of the frontier districts known as *pays d'états*. These areas had
been annexed at various periods since the later Middle Ages and
formed, in extent, about one-third of the national territory—the
rest of the country, the central core of the kingdom, being termed the
pays d'élections. The incorporation of the *pays d'états* had usually
been accompanied by special capitulations, which placed the relations of these provinces and the French crown on a semi-contractual
basis. In such districts, French kings had originally been led to preserve the local assemblies of estates where they already existed—as,
for example, in Dauphiné, Burgundy, Provence, and Brittany,
acquired respectively in 1349, 1477, 1481 and 1532. Where, however,
the provincial estates had been divided among themselves, or had

1. For Physiocrats see note on p. 19.
2. For provincial estates, see below pp. 17–19.

offered systematic opposition to the Crown, they had been allowed to lapse. Thus the estates of Auvergne, Périgord, Guienne, Normandy, Dauphiné and Franche Comté had ceased to be summoned during the course of the seventeenth century. By the reign of Louis XVI provincial estates had survived only in Provence, Burgundy, Béarn, Brittany and Languedoc and were, in fact, only functioning effectively in the last two areas.

Nevertheless, the continued existence of the provincial estates in the eighteenth century was important for several reasons. In those parts of the country where the local estates continued to meet periodically, responsibility for local administration was shared with the agent of the central government, or *intendant*. In such areas there was thus greater scope for the exercise of local initiative, particularly in the field of road and transport improvement and in the planning of public works. The authority of the *intendant*, virtually unchallenged in the *pays d'élections*, was, in the *pays d'états*, subject to the moderating influence of the permanent officials or commissions of the local estates. Secondly, the local estates had certain fiscal privileges which they had been able successfully to defend when assailed by reforming finance ministers. The amount of royal taxation to be levied in the *pays d'états* was made the subject of discussion and bargaining between the representatives of the estates and the officials of the treasury and the estates had the option of making fixed annual grants or *abonnements* in the case of new taxes, which enabled them to evade their full liability. The assessment and collection of state taxation was also left to the fiscal agents of the estates, with the result that, in Languedoc, the *taille* was assessed, not arbitrarily as in the *pays d'élections*, but on landed property. Special local taxes were also voted in the estates to meet local expenditure, which tended to be much higher than in the rest of the country. The financial credit of the provincial estates, resting on a sound budgetary basis, was assured, and the national treasury not infrequently found it necessary to rely on local loans raised through their agency.

Thirdly, it is essential to recognise that these local institutions, although progressive in their economic and administrative policy, were controlled by the lay or clerical aristocracy. This was true even in Languedoc, where the members of the third estate had as many votes in the assembly as those of the clergy and nobility combined and where even the voting was by head, and not by order. In Languedoc the preponderant role in the local estates was played by the upper clergy, in Brittany by the lay nobility. As the primate of

Languedoc, the archbishop of Narbonne was *ex officio* president of the assembly and, in the intervals between the annual meetings, the main channel of communication with the central government. It was the archbishop who nominated the members of the commissions, which prepared detailed administrative proposals for ratification in the plenary assemblies. The clergy of Languedoc was represented in the estates by its twenty bishops and three archbishops, and these invariably presided over and acted as spokesmen for the preparatory commissions. The lay nobility in the estates consisted of twenty-three 'barons' who sat in their own right and took only a limited part in the proceedings. The majority of the members of the third estate held seats in the assembly *ex officio*, as mayors of the chief towns of the province. Even the elected members of this estate represented only close municipal oligarchies and the third estate as a whole exercised no initiative and usually followed the lead given by the bishops. In Brittany, the estates met only once every other year, the number of lay nobles sitting and voting in the assembly rarely sank below five hundred, whereas there were less than fifty representatives of the third estate. The influence of the upper clergy was much less pronounced than in Languedoc, and the proceedings were dominated by the lay nobility, which had a contemporary reputation for turbulence and disaffection.

The existence of these institutions provided the lay and clerical nobility with the opportunity of playing an effective part in the conduct of local affairs at least in the *pays d'états*. In relation to the central government, however, the estates tended to be reactionary and conservative and reluctant to submit to any reforms designed to weaken or destroy their financial or political privileges.

(iv) *Agrarian distress*

In the latter part of the eighteenth century, the French peasants were almost as unprogressive in economic matters as the nobility were reactionary in politics. This was because they considered that the progress of scientific agriculture would jeopardise their accustomed means of livelihood. Although that movement had the blessing of the enlightened school of Physiocratic economists and the backing of the government, its chief beneficiaries were the wealthy and privileged land-holders.[1] The agrarian problem in France at this period, indeed, arose mainly from the clash between the monarchy's

1. The Physiocrats were a coterie of writers on economic theory who believed that the true and unique source of national wealth was agriculture.

efforts to improve agricultural productivity and the determination
of the peasants to retain their traditional methods of cultivation and
communal rights.

Shortly after the middle of the century, a powerful current of
opinion in favour of the capitalistic development of French agriculture had been stimulated by scientific interest in the new methods
of husbandry popularised in England by Jethro Tull, by the economic
writings of the Physiocrats and by the practical experiments of
powerful nobles who had been exiled from the court for political
reasons. The Physiocrats clearly grasped that among the causes of the
recurrent famines, from which France suffered in the eighteenth
century, were not only the inadequate system of communications,
but also the reluctance of the peasants to release their stocks of corn
for sale in areas where shortages were more pronounced. The
Physiocrats also advocated the long-term increase in corn prices, in
order to stimulate agricultural production, but such a policy had no
attraction for the peasants who were mostly subsistence farmers. Nor
did the peasants approve the Physiocratic encouragement of enclosure
and the division of the common lands, since the former required
capital which they did not possess, while the latter involved them in the
loss of their collective rights. The peasants failed also to understand
how their interests would be served by the Physiocratic programme
of fiscal equality by means of a single but universal tax on land.

The new economic policy on the other hand, had a powerful
appeal to local administrators, vexed by the difficulties of maintaining public order during agricultural crises, to the government,
because it seemed to offer a solution to the problem of unbalanced
budgets, and to the great landed proprietors, who were anxious to
increase their revenues, owing to the rising cost of court life at Versailles. Government interest in Physiocratic ideas was shown, after
1761, by the establishment of a special Agricultural Committee, with
Bertin as minister at its head, and by the encouragement throughout
the kingdom of agricultural societies, devoted to the inculcation of
the new scientific methods. Royal decrees were promulgated per-
mitting enclosure and royal ministers, such as Turgot and Calonne,
made efforts to break down the state regulation of corn prices and
marketing conditions.

Inevitably, this activity conflicted with the views and interests of
the French peasants. Long before the revolution of 1789, the French
peasant was personally free, and he had also often become an owner-
occupier of the soil. There can be little doubt, however, that the

majority of the rural inhabitants of France were wretchedly impoverished. It is now agreed by historians that, in the later years of
the *ancien régime*, the peasants 'owned', on the average, between 30
and 40 per cent of the French soil. Yet their real position can be
understood only if the extraordinary diversity in their social and
economic conditions is taken into account, and only if it is realised
that the livelihood of very few of them was at any time secure. As
Arthur Young later discovered, large-scale cultivation in France
was the exception. The large proprietors usually leased out their
land in return for fixed money rents, as was the normal practice
in the area north of Paris, or, alternatively, in return for a share in
the crop. The latter system, known as *métayage*, obtained in two-
thirds of the country, predominantly in the centre and south and
wherever the vine was cultivated.[1] Alongside the peasant proprietor,
therefore, were ranged the tenant-farmer, the share-cropper (*métayer*),
individuals who partly owned their land and partly rented it and
also rural day-labourers, chiefly dependent on their wages, but sometimes eking out their existence by means of a small holding on a
rental tenure. In some regions, such as maritime Flanders or the
neighbourhood of Versailles, heads of families who were neither
owner-occupiers nor tenant-farmers constituted between 70 and 75
per cent of the population. In Lower Normandy, at least 33 per cent
of the inhabitants belonged to the same rural proletariat. When
work was scarce and the price of bread high, this class had no other
resource but to beg or to take to banditry. The vast majority of
peasant-proprietors and tenant-farmers, because of the inadequacy
of their holdings, usually had to engage in some form of rural by-
industry, or even, from time to time, work as agricultural day-
labourers. In other words, the economic position of most peasants,
on the eve of the revolution, was precarious in the extreme.

In these circumstances, the continued retention by the peasants
of their common rights—the right of common pasturage on the
open fields, the use of the commons, the right of gathering wood for
fuel in the forests, the right of gleaning and gathering stubble after
the harvest—was indispensable as a means of keeping body and soul
together. Some of these common rights—such as common pasturage
—involved the continuance of the rigid and traditional methods of

1. According to Arthur Young the normal contract was for the landlord to find half
the cattle and half the seed, and the *métayer* found the labour and implements and
paid the taxes. The crop was usually divided half and half. There was, however, a good
deal of local variation in the contracts.

cultivation; others, such as the right of gleaning, handicapped cultivators at harvest time because custom prescribed the use of the sickle
instead of the scythe.[1] In general, the peasants were fanatically
opposed to enclosure and to the division of the commons, since such
processes benefited the large proprietors exclusively, and they were
also opposed to the cultivation of new crops other than cereals. This
conservatism sprang essentially from the fact that the poorer cultivators were not interested in producing for the market, or in the
prospect of increasing national agricultural productivity. The tenant-farmers of the north violently condemned the consolidation of
holdings and, in Picardy, those who had taken up the holdings of
evicted tenants were subjected to veritable boycotting. In areas where
métayage was the normal practice, the main grievance of the peasants
was against the employment by the proprietors of managers or
'farmers-general', as they were called. Recourse to these individuals,
who were sometimes powerful financiers, and sometimes local
tradesmen, had first been made by the clergy, but, from the beginning
of the eighteenth century, the practice had become widespread. This
method of sub-letting was particularly necessary where *métayage*
was the rule, because owners found that, unless minute and careful
supervision was exercised, their *métayers* neglected their holdings to
work as day-labourers, or abandoned them without adequate
notice. Continual visits were also required to ensure that the crops
were properly divided and the conditions of the leases observed.
As the representatives of the owners, these sub-contractors often
behaved tyrannically. They were also unpopular because they were
suspected of being 'monopolists' in corn, and because their strict
accounting deprived the *métayers* of the prospect of any incidental
perquisites. Finally, it may be noted that the large class of agricultural
labourers was radically opposed to any efforts to break down the
state and municipal regulation of the corn trade, for this they regarded as essential to protect them, as consumers, from the activities
of corn-merchants, middlemen and speculators.

The second main source of peasant discontent was the employment
by the landlords of specialists in feudal law (*feudistes*) to revive
obsolete feudal claims and to bring up to date the manorial rolls
and records of feudal obligations (*terriers*).[2] This tendency was

1. The labourers preferred the sickle to the scythe because it gave them more
work and made gleaning more profitable.
2. The reality of this so-called 'feudal reaction' was questioned by Professor Aulard
in his book, *La Révolution française et le régime féodal*, Paris, 1919, and recent research
suggests that its importance may have been exaggerated.

partly the result of the system of sub-contracting to 'farmers-general' noted above, but it reflected also the need of the impoverished provincial nobility to increase their main source of income from feudal dues and the more business-like management of their landed property on the part of the newly created nobility of middle-class origin. The elaboration of the new manorial rent-rolls during the latter part of the eighteenth century was carried out at the expense of the peasants. The latter were also made responsible for declaring the extent of their holdings and, if subsequent investigation showed that the area had been underestimated, the excess was confiscated by the lord. If the peasants ventured to contest any of the new feudal claims their suits ultimately came for judgement before the local *parlements*, which usually could be depended upon to reject them. The claim was also advanced on behalf of the lords of the manor that, in law, the common lands were their property. Formal recognition of this claim was given by the monarchy whenever the division of the common lands occurred, for it became established usage to allot one-third of the lands so redistributed to the local lords. Thus there can be little doubt that the feudal system of land tenure in France not only became more indefensible but also more oppressive as the eighteenth century drew to its close.[1]

Finally, recent research, carried out by Professor C. E. Labrousse, has shown that the peasants were the worst sufferers from the eighteenth-century changes in the levels of general and relative prices.[2] The average general prices of consumers' goods in France were 45 per cent higher in the period 1771–89 and 65 per cent higher between 1785 and 1789 than they had been between 1726 and 1741. This long-term inflationary movement may be mainly attributed to the marked increase during the century in the amount of metallic currency in circulation, to the greater expansion of credit facilities, relatively to the production of marketable industrial products, and to the demand caused by a rapidly increasing population.[3] A study of relative prices reveals, moreover, that the cost of living rose more steeply for those who were living nearest to the subsistence level,

---

1. This 'feudal reaction' did not occur in the west of France, which may partly account for the absence of hostility to their feudal superiors among the peasants of La Vendée and Brittany.

2. See particularly his work *La Crise de l'Economie Française à la fin de l'Ancien Régime et au début de la Révolution*, Paris, 1944.

3. Between 1726 and 1780 France absorbed no less than half the stock of precious metals imported into Europe. The total population of France rose during the eighteenth century from 18,000,000 to 26,000,000.

than for the middle class or the rich. The poorer-quality cereals, for example—rye, buckwheat and maize—which formed the staple ingredients of the bread consumed by the peasants, rose more in price just before the revolution than did wheat. At the same period, average money wages rose only by 22 per cent, so that, taken in the mass, French wage earners saw their purchasing power fall by over a quarter.

Within this long-term upward movement of general prices there was, however, between 1776 and 1787 a period when the prices of agricultural products declined. Agricultural rents, which between 1758 and 1776 had risen more slowly than agricultural prices, subsequently remained stable and even tended to rise, so that in the new adverse conditions the profit margins of the tenant-farmers disappeared. It is true that the lords, as receivers of feudal dues in kind, also suffered during this period of agricultural recession, but they protected themselves by means of the 'feudal reaction'. One of the few agricultural products whose price continued to rise after 1776 was meat, but it was only the larger landed proprietors who were stock-breeders. When the smaller tenant-farmers attempted to change over to cattle-rearing their activities were frustrated by a severe fodder crisis in 1785. This agricultural recession was accompanied by a slump in the textile industries, which had been starved of their supplies of cotton during the American war, and which the fodder crisis deprived of wool. By 1788, moreover, the effects of English competition under the Anglo-French free trade treaty of 1786 had put further obstacles in the way of the textile trades and serious unemployment both in town and country was the result.

Thus, in 1787 and 1788, France was facing not only an unprecedented financial and political crisis, but also an economic crisis of the first magnitude.

2

THE REVOLT OF THE NOBILITY (1787–8)

(i) *Calonne's plans for radical reform*

The prolonged and embittered struggle between the monarchy and the nobility, which occupied the years 1787 and 1788, was precipitated by the attempt of the Finance Minister Calonne to solve France's mounting financial difficulties by comprehensive fiscal, economic and administrative reforms. As leading minister of the Crown since November 1783, Calonne had devoted himself to the task of overcoming the financial and credit crisis into which France had been plunged by her intervention in the War of American Independence. He had reinstituted a sinking-fund in order to provide for the regular redemption of the funded debt; he had carried out a much needed recoinage of the gold currency; and, by an extended use of public works, he had given a stimulus to industrial enterprise. In the course of these operations he had discovered the existence of the annual deficit which, as early as 1769, amounted to 70,000,000 *livres*. The drastic economies of his predecessors, Terray and Turgot, had reduced this gap between annual revenue and expenditure to 37,000,000 but, by the end of the American war, the deficit had risen again to 80,000,000. By 1786 the position had become even worse, for a prolonged investigation of the national finances indicated that, in 1787, the annual deficit would amount to 112,000,000 *livres*. In addition, short-term loans, contracted since 1776 and due for redemption between 1787 and 1797, amounted to about 400,000,000 *livres*.

In the spring of 1786 Calonne became convinced that only speedy and drastic action would suffice to save France from national bankruptcy. In this view, the minister had been confirmed by the refusal

of the *parlement* of Paris, in December 1785, to approve further
government borrowing. A 'new deal' in French finance was, by that
time, long overdue, and a convenient opportunity for it was offered
by the expiry in December 1786 of the contract for the collection of
the indirect taxes and by the termination of the third twentieth.[1]
On 20 August 1786, Calonne submitted to the king a preliminary
sketch of his proposals. The characteristic features of these plans
were that they involved a comprehensive overhaul not only of the
taxation structure, but also of the administrative machinery of the
French state and recourse to a quasi-representative national assembly. The proposals themselves, although not original, were based
upon an acute diagnosis of the existing deficiencies of the *ancien
régime* and offered a solution which might well have averted financial
and political collapse.

Calonne's approach to the problem of the deficit was to suggest
that government expenditure should be reduced by 20,000,000, that
the redemption of the short-term debt should be spread over twenty
instead of ten years, and that the revenue from the existing stamp
duty should be increased by extending it to a fresh range of official
documents and to provinces which had hitherto been exempt. He
calculated that, in this way, the gap between revenue and expenditure
would be reduced to 47,000,000. This he proposed to close by substituting for the two twentieths levied on land a direct tax on all landowners without exception.[2] To avoid the necessity of a costly and
protracted land survey, and to ease the burden on the peasant
owners, Calonne suggested that the new tax should be collected not
in money but in kind. The tax was to be a proportional one, and thus
its yield would fluctuate according to changes in agricultural productivity. It would also be graduated, in order to ensure greater dis-
tributive justice between the poorer and richer agricultural areas.
To this end, Calonne proposed to establish throughout France,
except in the *pays d'états*, elective parochial assemblies of local
landowners, which were to classify the land for taxation purposes
into four categories on the basis of its rental value. The net result of
these changes would be to increase the yield of taxation on land by
50,000,000 and thus to extinguish the long-standing annual deficit.

Calonne realised, however, that this solution of the country's

1. The third *vingtième*, which had been imposed in 1782 to redeem the American
debt, was to be extinguished in December 1786.
2. The first *vingtième*, imposed in 1749, had no fixed term. The second *vingtième*,
imposed in 1760, was due to lapse in December 1790.

immediate financial difficulties would need to be reinforced by measures designed to increase France's general productivity. Prominent among his plans for liberating French economic development was a scheme to abolish the internal customs barriers. The internal customs duties or *traites* were to disappear as from 1 October 1787. In their place, a moderate and uniform customs tariff on imports and exports was to be established at the national frontier and, finally, in order to stimulate the *entrepôt* trade, nominal duties only were to be levied on goods in transit and re-exported articles. These changes would make possible a radical reform of the government salt and tobacco monopolies and the suppression of a number of complex and unremunerative excise duties, which were hindering the development of important home industries. They would, also, have converted France into one of the largest areas of internal free trade in Europe and would not have involved the treasury in any loss of net revenue.

The minister had inducements to offer not only to the commercial, but also to the agricultural classes. In order to stimulate the transition to large-scale scientific farming on the English model, Calonne proposed to relax state control not only of the internal trade in corn but, under certain conditions, the export trade as well. Hitherto, the export of corn, once prices had risen to a certain height, had been automatically prohibited. In future, this embargo would apply as a local restriction in those provinces only which specifically requested its enforcement. This scheme, designed in the interests of the larger cultivators, was combined with measures to deal with local grain shortages as soon as they gave rise to public anxiety. Nor did Calonne neglect the grievances of the smaller agricultural producers. The three most oppressive state burdens which the peasants had to shoulder under the *ancien régime* were the *taille*, the *corvée* and the *gabelle* and, although Calonne could not see his way to abolishing these exactions outright, he brought forward plans which would have considerably reduced their incidence upon the labouring population. As regards the salt tax (*gabelle*), economies in its cost of collection would have been enforced and the minister devised a scheme which would have allowed salt smuggling to be eliminated. It was his intention that the *corvée* (or forced labour-service) should be commuted for a money payment and that the amount of revenue raised from the *taille* (or main direct tax) should be reduced by one-tenth. Finally, he suggested that small agriculturalists should be given the opportunity of acquiring portions of the royal domain lands either

by becoming tenants-in-chief of the Crown, or by holding the land
on a perpetual leasehold tenure. Previously leaseholders of domain
lands had only been granted leases of nine years' duration, which
were liable to be terminated at short notice by Crown resumptions.

The success of these financial and economic plans involved a
complete remodelling of local government in the *pays d'élections*.
In all villages of 1,000 inhabitants and over the minister proposed
to establish parochial assemblies consisting of rural proprietors,
whose annual income from land amounted to 600 *livres*. These
bodies were to classify the land for assessment under the new land-
tax, distribute poor relief and supervise public works. The next
stage of the new administrative hierarchy was to be formed by district
assemblies, vested with the responsibility of apportioning royal
taxes among the towns and villages and with the power to present
petitions on matters of local interest to newly created provincial
assemblies. These were to constitute the central hub of the machinery
of local government. To avoid any immediate challenge to the
surviving provincial estates, the provincial assemblies were not to
be extended to the *pays d'états* and were to represent not a province
but a *généralité*.[1] There are three points to notice about these provincial assemblies. First, Calonne put forward the revolutionary
proposal that, in these institutions, the hallowed distinction between
the separate 'orders' or 'estates' should be obliterated. Secondly,
it was an essential part of Calonne's schemes that the provincial
assemblies should possess advisory functions only and their executive
powers were, accordingly, confined to a narrow range of matters of
local significance. Thirdly, Calonne subjected their activities to
the close control of the agents of the central government—the *intendants*. The reform was designed, in other words, to achieve not so
much effective decentralisation as greater administrative uniformity.

The scope and significance of these plans were far-reaching.
Calonne's proposals would have radically altered the political,
social and economic structure of the *ancien régime* and, if implemented, would have anticipated a good deal of the legislative reforms
of the Constituent Assembly. By means of the new land-tax the
Crown would have been provided with what it most needed in the
eighteenth century—namely, an expanding revenue from direct
taxation. The tax, moreover, would have been permanent and would
thus have relieved the monarchy from its political dependence upon
the *parlements*. Budgetary equilibrium, combined with a greater

1. The *généralité* was the fiscal area administered by the *intendant*.

measure of fiscal equality, would have been attained. To compensate the hitherto privileged classes for their increased liability to taxation on their landed wealth, Calonne offered three concessions. The first was a suggestion that the nobility should be excused from the payment of the poll-tax (*capitation*). The second was the continued exemption of the privileged classes from the *corvée*, after it had been commuted. The third was that the clerical debt should be redeemed. By these concessions, Calonne wished to make clear to the nobility that he was not attempting to achieve complete fiscal equality. Nevertheless, the principle of the fiscal immunity of the privileged orders would have been infringed and the means proposed for the redemption of the clerical debt involved the alienation of some of the feudal dues owned by the clergy.

The disregard of privileged status and social precedence in the new provincial assemblies would have deprived the lay and clerical nobility of the chance of exercising in the local government of the *pays d'élections* the preponderant influence which they still retained in the *pays d'états*. A sharp check would thus have been administered to the their political aspirations and to their social exclusiveness. The taxation of the clerical estates, the abolition of the church's power of bargaining with the treasury over the grant of benevolences and the gradual extinction of the clerical debt would have gravely compromised the corporate organisation of the Gallican Church. It would have ceased to be what it had hitherto been—a state within a state. Once the provincial assemblies had taken root, the popular esteem enjoyed by the provincial estates as the champions of regional liberties and the political independence of the *parlements* might well have been eclipsed. Instead of being, in Burke's phrase, 'a despotism rather in appearance than in reality', the Bourbon monarchy would have been converted into an enlightened and effective autocracy. France would have, at last, emerged as a unitary national state with a uniform and efficient administration. It remained to be seen, however, whether the existing government would be strong enough to execute the reforms if the privileged orders united to resist them.

If the plans were submitted, in the normal way, for the approval of the *parlement* of Paris, it was certain that they would encounter violent opposition. The summons of the national representative assembly, or States General, would on the other hand, have been generally interpreted as a confession of state bankruptcy and would have rendered speedy action to deal with the financial crisis difficult. In these circumstances, Calonne recommended that the reform pro-

gramme should be submitted to an assembly of Notables. The
members of this body would not be elected, but would be nominated
by the king: their functions would be purely advisory and they could
be instructed to discuss, not the substance of Calonne's proposals,
but merely the methods of putting them into operation. If the assembly ventured to criticise or oppose the reforms, it could be accused of
exceeding its powers, and could then be dismissed without loss of
prestige by the Crown.

Despite the opposition of the Chancellor Miromesnil, Louis XVI
approved Calonne's plans at the end of 1786 and decided to summon
an assembly of Notables early in 1787. The assembly which met at
Versailles on 22 February 1787 had a total membership of 144, with
thirty-six lay nobles, thirty-seven magistrates, twenty-six officers of
municipal corporations, fourteen prelates, twelve state counsellors,
an equal number of representatives of the provincial estates, and
seven princes of the blood. Less than thirty members of the assembly
belonged to the third estate.

(ii) *The revolt of the Notables*

The proceedings of this fateful assembly soon made it clear, however,
that Calonne had gravely miscalculated. He counted too confidently
on the support of the king and under-estimated the self-interest and
political resource of the clerical and judicial aristocracy. Calonne
had powerful enemies both at court and in the assembly itself—
among them d'Aligre, first magistrate of the *parlement* of Paris, and
de Brienne, archbishop of Toulouse, who was anxious to displace
him as first minister. In his opening exposition of the financial
situation Calonne revealed the existence, but not the amount, of the
large annual deficit, and showed how it had been increased by Necker's financial mismanagement of the American war. This challenge
to the celebrated *Compte rendu* of 1781 antagonised the strong
Neckerite faction in the assembly. As soon as the Notables began
the discussion of the minister's detailed proposals, opposition led
by the higher clergy and magistracy broke out. The schemes for the
emancipation of the corn trade, for the commutation of the *corvée*
and for the reform of the *taille* were accepted without much comment, since these did not threaten the interests of the aristocracy.
The plan for the redemption of the clerical debt, on the other hand,
was condemned as an attack on property, and the clergy pressed for
the matter to be referred to a forthcoming meeting of the clerical
assembly. Though the reforms in local government were accepted

in principle, criticism fastened upon the subordination of the provincial assemblies to the *intendants*, their limited powers and the abolition of the distinction between the separate 'orders'.

From these harassing tactics the Notables passed on to bitter and unrestrained attacks on Calonne's fiscal proposals. The Notables condemned the land-tax as both unconstitutional and unnecessary. In their view, the tax was unconstitutional because its duration and amount were not specified, and because it infringed the immunities of privileged corporations and provinces. They also contended that the necessity for the tax could not be established until Calonne placed his financial accounts before the assembly. These criticisms were obviously designed to wreck the minister's whole scheme of financial and administrative reform and to saddle Calonne with the sole responsibility for the disordered state of the finances. All Calonne's efforts to surmount this opposition came to grief. When the Notables refused to accept the subordinate role which had been assigned to them, the minister met his critics half-way by divulging the amount of the deficit and attempted to divide the assembly by making overtures to the clerical faction. His refusal, however, to allow an inquiry into the accuracy of Necker's *Compte rendu*, or to alter the character of the land-tax from a proportional to a fixed duty compromised the chances of any negotiated settlement. In desperation, Calonne appealed from the assembly to outside public opinion. When this attempt miscarried at the end of March, the minister found that he could no longer control the Notables and, on 8 April, as a result of court intrigues, fomented by de Brienne, he was dismissed and shortly afterwards exiled to his estates in Lorraine.[1]

Calonne's disgrace was a triumph for the opposition groups in the assembly. It indicated that any further effort to push through the reform schemes would succeed only if effective financial control were surrendered to the Notables, and if attention were paid to the political views of the aristocracy. Accordingly, at the end of April 1787, the king resolved to make a series of important concessions. The Notables were informed that the traditional precedence of the privileged orders would not be challenged in the new provincial assemblies, that the problem of the clerical debt would be referred for decision to the general assembly of the clergy, that the financial accounts would be communicated to the Notables and, finally, that the total yield of the projected land-tax would be fixed in relation

1. In August 1787, after legal proceedings had been started against him in the *parlement* of Paris, Calonne withdrew to England and thus became the first *émigré*.

to the amount of the outstanding deficit, once this had been verified. The task of implementing these promises was entrusted to Calonne's successor, de Brienne. The intriguing archbishop, however, soon found that success had so encouraged the Notables that their political pretensions had been magnified and their willingness to compromise extinguished. When they had satisfied themselves that Calonne had not over-estimated the deficit, they pressed for a more rigid control of departmental expenditure, the annual publication of the national accounts, and a regular system of treasury audit. This supervision should, they argued, be entrusted to an independent Finance Council, on which the Notables themselves should be represented. It was hardly to be expected that the government would agree with the necessity for such arrangements. Brienne, moreover, soon revealed his incapacity to devise financial remedies of his own. His proposals, submitted to a conference of the Notables on 9 May, represented merely a slightly modified form of those already suggested by Calonne. Virtually the only concession he had to offer was the fixing of the revenue to be raised from the land-tax at the figure of 80,000,000 *livres* a year. He also asked for an immediate loan of 50,000,000 to ensure the prompt repayment of the floating debt, a further extension of the stamp duty, and the introduction of a capitation tax based on household rents. The reply of the Notables was to insist that such fiscal proposals would require either the sanction of the *parlement* of Paris, or, more significantly, of the States General. Further discussion was now seen to be useless and on 25 May the assembly of Notables was dissolved. The monarchy had thus sustained a resounding defeat at the hands of the aristocracy. The financial problem was still unsolved and everything now turned on whether Brienne could persuade or intimidate the *parlement* of Paris.

(iii) *The revolt of the* parlements

It would probably have been better for the government if the struggle with the powerful Parisian magistrates, which Calonne had sought to avoid and which the Notables had rendered inevitable, could now have been decided. Such was the advice tendered by the new Keeper of the Seals, Lamoignon. Brienne, however, was reluctant to seek the registration of the revised reform edicts *en bloc*, for fear of provoking an immediate quarrel with the *parlement*. Instead, he decided to obtain the approval of the less contentious measures first, in the hope that the political atmosphere would subsequently clear. This procedure soon proved unprofitable. By 28 June, it is true, the draft schemes for the establishment of the provincial assemblies, for the liberation of the corn trade and for the commutation of the *corvée* were all duly registered. The delay in presenting the fiscal edicts, however, enabled the opposition groups in the *parlement* of Paris to organise their forces. It was soon apparent that the magistrates had determined to imitate the highly successful tactics elaborated by the Notables. As soon as the stamp and land-tax proposals were presented for registration in the course of July, the magistrates countered by demanding the communication of the fiscal accounts. When these were refused by the government, on the ground that they had already been revealed to the Notables, the *parlement* declared itself incompetent to sanction taxes whose duration had not been fixed, and sought to embarrass Brienne by clamouring for the summons of the States General. On 26 July the stamp duty was rejected and on 30 July the land-tax was also refused. Brienne had, therefore, no alternative but to proceed to an enforced registration of these measures by means of a *lit de justice* on 6 August. The magistrates condemned this measure as unconstitutional, declared the decrees invalid and on 10 August, on the motion of Duport, instituted criminal proceedings against Calonne for financial malpractices. These proceedings were, in turn, quashed by the government and the *parlement* of Paris was exiled to Troyes on 15 August.

The next stage in the contest was begun by a crisis in French foreign policy, which gravely affected the credit of the ministry and the prestige of the monarchy. Partly because of Dutch colonial losses to Great Britain during the American War of Independence, and partly because of the Stattholder's English connexions, bitter political strife was at this time raging between the House of Orange and the Dutch republican party of so-called 'Patriots'.[1] In 1786 the Stattholder William V had been suspended from his position as Captain General and civil war in the United Provinces appeared imminent. In this struggle, the Stattholder looked for support to his brother-in-law, Frederick William II of Prussia, and to Great Britain, whose ambassador, Sir James Harris, was anxious to break down the close connexions between the 'Patriots' and France. In June 1787 an incident occurred which made the Dutch domestic issue an international one. This was the arrest of the Stattholder's wife by volunteer troops of the 'Patriot' party, as she was travelling from Nymwegen to the Hague, with the intention of rallying political backing for the Orange cause. The leading Prussian minister, Hertzberg, was,

1. William V's mother was a daughter of George II.

at this time, concerned to end his country's diplomatic isolation by means of an understanding with Great Britain, which he hoped would facilitate his schemes in eastern Europe against Austria and Russia. He seized on the Dutch crisis as a means of accomplishing these objectives and persuaded Frederick William to intervene in Holland, after receiving British assurances of assistance if France interfered. On 13 September 1787, Prussian troops crossed the Dutch border and went to the assistance of the Orange party. Montmorin, the French foreign minister, who had led the Patriots to expect help was, however, deterred from fulfilling his promises, partly owing to the financial crisis, partly by British representations and partly because France's ally, Austria, had been drawn into a Russo-Turkish war in eastern Europe. France threatened to concentrate troops on the frontier, but the only result was the conclusion of an Anglo-Prussian alliance early in October. Confronted by this un-expected combination, the French ministry was compelled, on 28 October, to make a humiliating repudiation of its previous pledges to the Dutch republicans. France's influence in the United Provinces and its prestige in Europe were thus compromised. Early in 1788 a Triple Alliance between Great Britain, the United Provinces and Prussia guaranteed the position of the restored House of Orange.

The impact of the Dutch crisis upon French domestic politics was threefold. It led to the resignation of the departmental heads of the War Office (de Ségur) and of the Admiralty (de Castries), both of whom had wished to give active assistance to the 'Patriot' party; it drew public attention once more to the desperate financial situation, and thus increased the general conviction that the summons of the States General was indispensable; it also persuaded Brienne of the necessity of reaching an accommodation with the recalcitrant magis-trates. Brienne offered to recall the *parlementaires* to the capital, on condition that they agreed to the prolongation and increase of the twentieths and to the taxation of the clergy. Although the king had agreed at the end of August to confer the title of Principal Minister on Brienne, in order to reinforce his authority over his colleagues, the archbishop was not in a strong position in his negotiations with the judges. When the *parlement* replied that it would only consent to the prolongation of the twentieths till 1792 in their existing form, the minister hastened to accept. This bargain was struck on 19 Sep-tember, a week after the Prussian invasion of the United Provinces. The compromise had thus been clearly dictated by the accumulating difficulties which threatened to overwhelm the ministry. Mutual suspicion, however, remained and the compromise was an uneasy one, since it involved both sides in self-contradictions. The *parlement* had now sponsored the raising of taxes which it had so recently declared it was incompetent to approve, while Brienne had surrendered the projects which he, like Calonne, had defended as indispensable to financial salvation and fiscal equality.

There still remained the problem of the short-term debt, and to justify a loan of 420,000,000 *livres* spread over five years, Brienne proposed a new plan of reform for the achievement of financial equilibrium by 1792 without recourse to the States General in the intervening period. Luckily for Brienne, certain of the more powerful magistrates, led by the conservative Duval d'Espréménil, were now apprehensive of a declaration of state bankruptcy and of popular disorders. In this situation a new bargain was suggested. The *parlement* agreed to sanction the loan in return for a definite promise from the king to summon the States General. Brienne submitted and the king's hesitations were overcome by Lamoignon's arguments that the royal legislative independence would not be endangered, since the States General could only present petitions and could not exercise the initiative. On 18 November, the Principal Minister announced that a *royal session* of the *parlement* would be held the following day.[1] At this meeting, Lamoignon explained that the king had agreed to summon the States General for 1792, provided that, in the interval, the government was allowed to float the required loan. The chancellor then emphasised that the national assembly, when it did meet, would possess merely advisory functions and that it would be nothing more than an enlarged king's council. This view provoked furious protests from the magistrates and when Lamoignon turned the proceedings into a *lit de justice*, in order to secure the enforced registration of the loan, the duke of Orléans, one of the princes of the blood, formally protested in the name of the peers that this procedure was illegal. The king's reply was to exile the duke to his estates and imprison two of the leading opposition magistrates—the abbé Sabatier de Cabre and Fréteau.

Once more a position of stalemate had resulted, but early in 1788, in the final stage of the conflict, both sides began to prepare for decisive action. In January Duval launched a campaign against the use of *lettres de cachet* and the whole process of arbitrary arrest and imprisonment. In April the *parlement* renewed its remonstrances

1. In a *royal session*, as distinct from a *lit de justice*, the magistrates were allowed to express their views on royal edicts, but not to vote.

against the enforced registration of the loan but was reminded by the
King that, if he yielded, the monarchy would be converted into 'an
aristocracy of magistrates, which would be as contrary to the rights
and interests of the nation, as to his own sovereign prerogatives',
This was new and unfamiliar doctrine in the mouth of a technically
absolute monarch, but both sides had now realised that the duel
between autocracy and aristocracy was being fought in the presence
of the third estate. On 3 May, on the motion of Duval d'Esprémenil,
the *parlement* formulated a declaration of Fundamental Laws, in
which it included the right of the nation freely to consent to taxation
in the States General, the sanctity of the customs and capitulations
of the separate provinces and the principle of the irremovability of
the judges. Although some historians have seen in this declaration
an anticipation of the more famous declaration of the Rights of
Man, it represented in truth the views of the conservative legal
aristocracy and the interests of provincial separatism. In one respect
the declaration did set a precedent which was followed in the constitutional struggles of 1789. Anticipating the imminent dissolution
of their corporation, the magistrates took a collective oath not to
serve in any other legal body which might be established in its place
and placed the constitutional principles solemnly enunciated in the
declaration in the safe keeping of the king, the peers, and the States
General. It was this procedure which was imitated by Mounier and
the other lawyers who drafted the Tennis Court Oath of 20 June
1789. Brienne and Lamoignon had, meanwhile, completed their
plans for striking down the political power of the judges. Orders
were given for the arrest of their leaders, d'Esprémenil and Goislard
de Montsabert, on the night of 4 May. When the two champions of
judicial independence sought refuge in the *parlement*, the Palace of
Justice at Paris was surrounded by armed forces. The assembled
magistrates refused to designate their colleagues to the marquis
d'Agoult, the officer sent to arrest them, and it was only at the end
of a thirty-hour session that d'Esprémenil and Montsabert finally
surrendered after solemn protests against the arbitrary proceedings
of the government. On 8 May the long expected blow fell, when Louis
XVI, in a *lit de justice* held at Versailles, enforced the registration of
six edicts, designed by Lamoignon to restrict the judicial and to
destroy the political powers of the *parlements*. The power of registering royal edicts applying to the country as a whole was transferred
from the *parlements* to a so-called 'Plenary Court', whose constitution suggested that it would prove a pliable instrument in the hands

of the government. The judicial component of this institution consisted of the senior judges of the *parlement* of Paris and the president and one other magistrate from each of the provincial *parlements*—in other words of judges who were the law officers of the Crown. Apart from these magistrates, the court was to be composed of princes of the blood, peers of France, court officials and leading representatives of the church, the army and civil service. The purely judicial competence of the *parlements* was considerably narrowed by the establishment of forty-seven 'Grand Bailliwicks'. These tribunals were meant to absorb the greater part of the appellate jurisdiction of the *parlements* in both civil and criminal cases, and thus to render possible a radical reduction in the number of magistrates. The edicts also made great inroads upon the numerous forms of private jurisdictions in the hands of the aristocracy. And, finally, important reforms were made in the sphere of criminal procedure. The last vestiges of torture, applied to condemned criminals in order to compel them to betray their accomplices, now disappeared. The *parlements* were not abolished, as they had been in 1771, but they were to be deprived in future of all power of opposing the monarchy's programme of social and fiscal reform. If Calonne had dealt with the magistrates in this way, instead of having recourse to the assembly of Notables, the whole course of French history might have been altered. In 1788 Lamoignon's *coup d'état* came too late, and its result was to provoke widespread revolt in the provinces.[1]

(iv) *The revolt of the provinces*

There can be little doubt that these reforms would have made French justice speedier and more uniform, but they were represented by the magistrates as a device to delay the summons of the States General and as an attack on provincial liberties. Substance had been given to the latter charge by Brienne's final arrangements for the establishment of the provincial assemblies. The government had prescribed that half the members of these assemblies should, in the first instance, be nominated by the king, had conceded to the third estate double representation and had arranged that the separate orders should vote in common. By these regulations the government succeeded in antagonising the local aristocracy and in weakening the position of the *intendants*. Resistance to the new institutions took two forms—attempts by local *parlements*, particularly those of

1. For the whole subject of the revolt of the magistrates see J. Egret, *La Pré-Révolution Française*, 1787–1788, Paris, 1962.

Bordeaux and Toulouse, to wreck the whole administrative experiment, and a campaign in Hainault, Provence and Dauphiné to revive the provincial estates. This agitation still continued when Lamoignon's attack on the *parlements* in May 1788 stimulated further ill-feeling in the provinces. It is significant that the main disturbances caused by the judicial reforms occurred in Béarn, Brittany and Dauphiné. These were areas where the magistrates found it easy to incite popular disorders because they could appeal to provincial separatism and to the aristocratically controlled provincial estates. In the course of May the *parlements* of Pau and Rennes stirred up the local population to violent demonstrations against the *intendants* and military commanders on the spot, and threatened the Government with civil war. On 7 June a historic outbreak in Dauphiné in sympathy with the exiled magistrates of the *parlement* of Grenoble set the pattern for further disturbances. Though the bloodshed in these revolts was only on a small scale, the situation in the provinces was visibly getting out of control. Military discipline could not be relied on and the executive appeared to be paralysed.[1]

Meanwhile Brienne, in Paris, found that national bankruptcy was looming nearer. In these straits, he turned for assistance, at the end of May, to an extraordinary meeting of the Clerical Assembly. This body, however, passed remonstrances condemning Lamoignon's judicial reforms, threw its weight behind the agitation for the summons of the States General and voted only 1,800,000 *livres* as a *don gratuit* instead of the 8,000,000 requested by the treasury. Confronted by this united opposition of the judicial, lay and clerical aristocracy, Brienne was compelled to surrender. On 5 July 1788, the Principal Minister announced that the States General would be summoned and, on 8 August, fixed the date of its meeting at Versailles for 1 May 1789. Lamoignon's judicial reforms were, at the same time, suspended.

---

1. The following articles by Professor J. Egret throw new light on these provincia revolts: 'Les origines de la Révolution en Bretagne, 1788–9', *Revue Historique*, vol. CCXIII (1955); 'La Pré-Révolution en Provence, 1787–9', *Annales Historiques de la Révolution Française*, vol. XVI (1954); 'La révolution aristocratique en Franche-Comté et son échec, 1788–9', *Revue d'histoire moderne et contemporaine*, new series, vol. I (1954).

3

SOCIAL AND POLITICAL CONFLICTS ON
THE EVE OF THE REVOLUTION (1788–9)

(i) *Necker's second ministry and the recall of the* parlement

Lamoignon's comment on the check to his judicial reforms was that, as the aristocracy had dared to resist the king, there would soon be an end of the *parlement*, the nobility and the clergy. It was, however, Brienne's ministry which fell first. On 16 August the Prime Minister was compelled to suspend treasury payments till September, and to announce that, when payments were resumed, they would be made partly in the paper notes issued by the Discount Bank. Two days later, these notes were made inconvertible. In the existing circumstances, such pronouncements were hardly distinguishable from a declaration of national bankruptcy. Brienne's position was now untenable. The queen made last-minute efforts to save her favourite from disgrace, by trying to secure the co-operation of Necker as a financial expert. When Necker refused to serve under Brienne, the queen, acting on the advice of her confidential counsellor, the Austrian ambassador, induced the archbishop to resign on 25 August.

Necker was then recalled to power as Director-General of the Finances. The king disliked him as a protestant and a foreigner, and the queen realised that he would be difficult to control. Public opinion, however, regarded Necker as the only man capable of averting financial chaos and, from the moment he joined the ministry his position in it was preponderant. Unfortunately, he had none of the qualities of the true statesman and not even the determination of the successful politician. His prestige as a financier enabled him to avert national bankruptcy, but did not fit him to solve the constitutional issues raised by the summons of the States General or enable him to devise a political programme, which might have eased the transition from absolutism to limited monarchy.

In the usual eighteenth-century manner, Necker immediately reversed the policy of his predecessor—by recalling the *parlement* of Paris from exile. Arrangements were put in hand for the holding of a *lit de justice* with this object on 15 September. The magistrates objected to this procedure, however, and insisted on the dismissal of Lamoignon, the author of the May edicts and the one strong man in the government. Necker agreed that the summons of the States General should be advanced from 1 May to 1 January 1789, but stipulated that judicial reform should then be reconsidered. On this basis an understanding was reached, the king consenting to dispense with the *lit de justice*, Necker agreeing to drop Lamoignon, and the *parlements* accepting the restoration of their political powers as provisional. The agreement, nevertheless, proved unfortunate for both Necker and the magistrates. Necker secured the appointment, as Keeper of the Seals, of Barentin, the president of the *Cour des Aides*, a man of moderate ability whom he thought he would be able to dominate without difficulty. In fact, Barentin proved that he was no man of straw, and his strongly conservative views soon conflicted with those of Necker. This conflict was important because Barentin was officially responsible for supervising the arrangements for the meeting of the States General. Even more significant for the future was the manner in which the *parlement* of Paris registered the royal edict antedating the summons of the National Assembly. For, on 25 September, the magistrates made a public declaration that, in their view, the States General should be convoked and composed according to the forms of 1614.

The effect of this pronouncement on public opinion was immediate, for it revealed the political calculations which had inspired the aristocratic campaign for the summons of the National Assembly. If the estates were organised, as in 1614, with an equal number of representatives, and if each order voted separately, the clergy and the nobility would be able to enforce their will on the third estate. Outworn privileges would thus be protected and the monarchy and the country would be at the mercy of the reactionaries. The declaration of the *parlement* had, moreover, already been anticipated by the clerical assembly in June 1788. That body had expressed itself in favour of the strict separation of the estates, and had even reformulated the obsolete convention that the decisions of any two estates could not legally bind the remaining order. The clergy were clearly determined to protect their status as a privileged corporation, even though it were assailed by both the nobility and the third estate. By the end of September 1788 middle-class opinion, which had hitherto tamely supported the political campaign of the *parlements* against monarchical and ministerial 'despotism', realised that a formidable coalition of the lay, clerical and judicial aristocracy was already in being. The representation of the third estate in 1614 had consisted mainly of judicial members, mostly of magisterial rank, and had, moreover, also included members of the nobility. The proceedings of the national assembly in 1614 had been practically confined to the discussion of financial questions, and, owing to the separation of the estates, they had also been chaotic and inconclusive. For the *parlement* to ignore the social and economic development of the middle class, which had occurred during the last century and a half, and to press for the revival of the forms of 1614 was thus a man- œuvre, the purpose of which was unmistakable.

The consequences of the declaration of 25 September were, there- fore, far-reaching. Rivarol accused the magistrates, with some point, of 'having so far been unfaithful guardians who had abused the protracted minority of their dependants'. The popularity of the *parlements* collapsed overnight. Thus it was that, in the autumn and winter of 1788, the struggle between the monarchy and the aristocracy was transformed into a social and political conflict between the privileged and unprivileged classes. As the issues broadened, the solidarity of the privileged orders weakened. A split appeared even in the ranks of the *parlement* of Paris between the conservative magistrates and those with liberal inclinations, who soon came to be known as the 'Americans'. The third estate also found champions of its claims among the lay and clerical aristocracy. A significant change occurred in the tone of current political speculation, for at this point a number of French political theorists temporarily aban- doned the doctrines of Montesquieu, the defender of corporate privilege, in favour of those of Rousseau, the critic of all forms of association within the state. Lastly, there was formed in these months, in opposition to the coalition of the conservative aristoc- racy, a combination of liberal theorists and politicians who assumed the style of the 'patriotic' or 'national' party.

(ii) *The formation of the 'patriotic' party*

Among the latter, were members of the 'liberal' aristocracy, such as the duke de Rochefoucauld-Liancourt, the duke d'Aiguillon, the marquis de Lafayette, viscount de Noailles and counts Alexandre de Lameth, de Ségur and Clermont-Tonnerre. From the ranks of the higher clergy were recruited men such as Le Franc de Pompignan, archbishop of Vienne, Champion de Cicé, archbishop of Bordeaux, Boisgelin, archbishop of Aix, Lubersac, bishop of Chartres, and the abbé de Périgord, soon to become bishop of Autun, and known to history as Talleyrand. The group of progressive magistrates included, among others, Adrien Duport, Hérault de Séchelles and Le Pelletier de Saint-Fargeau. Bankers such as Laborde, barristers and jurists such as Target and Bergasse, writers such as Lacretelle, Volney, the the abbé Sieyès and the protestant pastor Rabaut de Saint-Étienne, *déclassé* nobles like Mirabeau and the opposition group centring round the duke of Orléans showed that the 'patriotic' party was in truth representative of the 'political' nation. Many of the 'liberal' aristocracy had fought as volunteers in the American war and some, like Lafayette, professed to believe in a hazy form of 'republicanism'. Most of the liberal prelates were ambitious 'administrative' bishops with ministerial aspirations. The progressive magistrates were, to some extent, moved by a desire to escape the unpopularity which had suddenly descended on their more reactionary colleagues. With these motives, however, there mingled, as events were to prove, a good deal of unselfishness, political idealism and devotion to the cause of liberalism.

The political activity of these groups was organised in the exclusive salons of Madame de Tessé, the Maréchale de Beauveau, and Madame de Genlis, in the popular coffee-houses of the Palais Royal and, above all, in the clubs which sprang into life in 1788 and 1789. Political clubs in France had first come into existence in the early eighties, largely in imitation of their English counterparts, but most of them had been closed by order of the government during the crisis of 1787. These now reappeared and fresh ones were formed, some with philanthropic objectives such as the *Société des Amis de Noirs*, sponsored by Brissot, others, like the *club de Viroflay*, the meeting-place of the liberal aristocracy at Versailles, in order to champion the cause of the third estate. Masonic lodges, affiliated to the parent lodge of the *Grand Orient*, founded by the duke de Montmorency-Luxembourg, also proliferated at this period. Freemasonry was still aristocratic, but the lodges helped to popularise the rationalist writings of the *philosophes* and also to promote the political intrigues of the Orléanist opposition. The most powerful influence at work, however, was the mysterious Committee of Thirty, founded in November

1788, which met at the house of the wealthy magistrate, Adrien Duport. This committee corresponded with agents of the middle class in the provinces, subsidised and circulated liberal political pamphlets and later played a great part in drawing up model instructions for the guidance of deputies of the third estate in the national assembly. It included all the most influential leaders of the 'patriotic' party—Lafayette, Mirabeau, Talleyrand, the abbé Sieyès, Condorcet, d'Aiguillon, La Rochefoucauld-Liancourt, de Castellane and de Noailles.

(iii) *Pamphlet warfare and the attack on privilege*

In announcing on 5 July the decision of the government to summon the States General, Brienne had appealed for information and advice on the historical precedents, to the country at large, and had in effect suspended, for this purpose at least, the censorship of the press. The result was a remarkable outburst of pamphlet literature. Among the brochures concerned with the nature and functions of the States General, it is only necessary here to mention the works of Target, Volney, Mounier, Rabaut Saint-Étienne, the count d'Antraigues and, above all, of Sieyès. Three fundamental ideas may be said to have emerged from these and other kindred works which were published in the winter of 1788–9—the idea of a declaration of rights, the conception of national sovereignty and the necessity of endowing France with a constitution. These concepts, which were so profoundly to influence the course and character of future events, represented the response of the third estate to the political challenge of the privileged orders. The campaign for a declaration of rights, embracing the pleas for equality and liberty, was the reply to the proclamation of the Fundamental Laws by the *parlement* of Paris in May 1788. The idea of the nation and of national sovereignty was meant to challenge the traditional hierarchical organisation of French society in separate orders or estates. The demand for a constitution was meant to refute the contention of the aristocratic traditionalists that France already possessed one. These ideas were best exemplified in the writings of Sieyès. His first pamphlet, 'Essay on Privileges', displayed the strongly egalitarian bias of all his political speculation, and was probably the product of his experience as a representative of the clergy in the provincial assembly of Orléans in 1787. The most famous and influential of all Sieyès' productions was, however, his brochure 'What is the Third Estate?' This was remarkable for the arresting slogans of its opening paragraphs, for its concise formulation of the political demands of the unprivileged classes, and for its identification of the third estate with the nation. Sieyès' thesis was contained in his answers to three questions which he posed at the outset of his inquiry. He demonstrated that the clergy was not strictly an estate of the realm at all, but a profession. He showed that the aristocracy was isolated from the rest of the community by privilege. He argued that the third estate constituted, by itself, the French nation. In the past, the third estate had been deprived of all political rights. In the future, it would demand to be at least 'something'. Its demands were, indeed, modest: that its representatives in the States General should be recruited exclusively from its own ranks, that the number of those representatives should equal in number those of the clergy and nobility combined, and that voting in the assembly should be, not by order, but by head. Not only did Sieyès crystallise the political programme of the third estate, he also outlined the methods by which its representatives in the States General of 1789 might succeed in achieving their objectives.[1] He advised them to take their stand on the principle, derived from Rousseau, that when drawing up the future constitution, the assembled representatives would possess unfettered legislative authority. Much was later to be heard of this so-called 'constituent' power.

(iv) *Necker and the convocation of the States General*

Meanwhile, the government, having staved off bankruptcy in the immediate future, had also turned its attention to the problem of organising the forthcoming meeting of the States General. In what sense would it pronounce its verdict—for or against the forms of 1614? Many of the constitutional issues which divided the estates in the spring and summer of 1789 might have been avoided if the government had made its own decision at this point, before the conflict between the privileged and unprivileged classes had become further embittered, while the popularity of the king was still unquestioned and the prestige of Necker undiminished. The matter had become more urgent because the date of the meeting of the national assembly had been advanced. This meant that some speedier method had to be devised of consulting informed opinion on the complicated issues involved than that contemplated by Brienne. Necker, conscious of the division of opinion in the ministry, decided to recall the Notables, and to consult their views. His hope was that he would be able to

---

1. *Vues sur les moyens d'exécution dont les représentants de la France pourront disposer en 1789.*

persuade the privileged orders voluntarily to sacrifice the traditional forms and immunities which had now been condemned by public opinion. The second assembly of Notables sat at Versailles from 6 November to 12 December 1788. Once again, the expectations of the government were not realised. Five out of the six working committees of the Notables rejected the claim of the third estate to 'double representation'. It was thus clear that the majority wished to make voting by order the invariable rule of procedure in the States General. The first committee, presided over by the king's brother, the count of Provence, accepted the idea of 'double representation' for the third estate by a majority of one, in order to make possible the holding of joint or common sessions of the orders in matters of general concern. One result of the 'patriotic' party's campaign in favour of the claims of the third estate was the recommendation of the Notables that all who possessed hereditary and transmissable nobility and all holders of ecclesiastical benefices should be allowed to vote in the elections to the States General. This was an obvious attempt to impress public opinion with the numerical size of the privileged orders. The suggestion was accepted by the government. Thus the clerical electorate comprised the whole body of the beneficed clergy and the result was that the bishops and archbishops elected to the national assembly were greatly outnumbered by the representatives of the lower clergy.

As the Notables broke up on 12 December, all the princes of the blood, with the exception of the count of Provence and the duke of Orléans, signed a manifesto condemning the pamphlet campaign in favour of the political pretensions of the third estate. This protest demanded that the agitation for 'double representation' should be dropped as the price of the nobility's offer to surrender its fiscal privileges and insisted that the existing constitution and the traditional form of the States General should be maintained intact. Meanwhile, Necker, by a private agreement with the Committee of Thirty and the liberal section among the magistrates, had persuaded the *parlement* of Paris to retract the September declaration approving the forms of 1614. In a new resolution, made public on 5 December, the *parlement* explained that its previous declaration related only to the method of summoning the States General and not to its composition. The latter issue was one to be determined by the king and the electors. The real point of the September declaration had been to urge on the government the desirability of basing the electoral constituencies on the units of judicial administration instead of on

fiscal areas. This explanation was accompanied by a petition to the
king urging him to draw up a new constitution incorporating the
principles of 'double' representation for the third estate, periodical
meetings of the States General, ministerial responsibility, guarantees
for individual liberty and a 'legitimate' liberty of the press. This
initiative failed entirely to recapture the previous popularity of the
parlement, but it did serve Necker's purpose in throwing into high
relief the grudging and retrograde attitude adopted by the Notables
and the princes of the blood.

The explosion of popular indignation which followed the pronouncements of the Notables confirmed Necker in his determination
to secure from the government at least the recognition of the principle of 'double' representation. His next step was, therefore, to disregard the views expressed by the Notables and to get this concession
approved by the royal council. Warnings had, by this time, begun
to come in from the *intendants* in the provinces that, if the political
claims of the unprivileged were rejected, civil war could speedily
ensue. If the financial problem were to be solved by the States General
some working alliance between the monarchy and the third estate
was essential. Necker determined to press on. In the course of discussions with his colleagues during December, it became clear that
while he could could count on the support of Montmorin, Saint-
Priest, La Luzerne, and possibly that of the duke de Nivernais, his
liberal policy would be strenuously opposed by Barentin and Puységur, the war minister. In this situation, the attitude of the king and
queen would be decisive, and although Louis continued to vacillate,
Marie Antionette made it understood that she, at least, would not
oppose Necker's suggestions. The queen, apparently, had still not
recovered from her indignation at the hostile attitude of the nobility
to the Crown in the crisis of 1787. The struggle in the royal council
was heated and prolonged. Necker offered to resign but, largely as
the result of the queen's support, he was finally able to secure the
council's consent to the concession of double representation for the
third estate. The decision was announced to the public on 27 December 1788, in the form of an act entitled 'Result of the Council'. This
prescribed that in the States General the third estate should have the
same number of representatives as the clergy and the nobility combined, but left unsettled the issue whether voting should take place
by order or by head.

Necker has often been criticised for not insisting on the necessity
of joint deliberation between the estates in the national assembly.

Even with the backing of the queen and of the count of Provence, however, the minister had only succeeded in gaining 'double' representation for the third estate with great difficulty and mainly by contending that it would not automatically entail voting in common, but merely render it possible. Greater firmness on his part would not have convinced the council and would, almost certainly, have alienated the count of Provence. Events were also to vindicate Necker's shrewd calculation that the grant of double representation would suffice for the moment, and that the third estate could safely be left to insist on the principle of common voting when the States General met. It is untrue to say that Necker had disregarded the issue completely, for in his unpublished report to the council Necker had explained that voting by order was the established practice and would continue to be legally binding, unless the procedure was altered with the sanction of the king and the common consent of all three estates. Nothing, however, was said on this matter in the public announcement of the council's decision. The view, therefore, gained currency that the method of deliberation and voting in the States General had been left as an open question. The result was unfortunate, for it caused the conflict between privileged and unprivileged to redouble in violence as the meeting of the national assembly drew nearer.

(v) *The elections to the States General*

The discussions had been so prolonged that the sessions of the States General had to be postponed from January to the end of April 1789 and the representatives did not actually meet till 4 May. The whole of January 1789 was taken up with the elaboration of the electoral arrangements. Although complicated, the final electoral regulations which appeared on 24 January were extremely liberal in scope. The electoral districts were formed out of the ancient territorial sub-divisions concerned with the administration of justice, the so-called bailliwicks. For the purpose of returning deputies, these areas were divided into principal and secondary bailliwicks. Traditional forms were also preserved with the decision that the deputies should be elected in separate orders. In the case of the privileged orders the regulations provided for direct universal suffrage. All the lay nobles, aged twenty-five and over, whether holders of fiefs or not, were entitled to attend the electoral assembly of their order in the bailliwick, either in person or by proxy. The bishops and parish priests exercised similar privileges in the electoral assemblies of the clergy, although canons and monks could only send representatives.

Deputies of the third estate, on the other hand, were chosen by a complicated system of indirect election. Except in Paris, where the vote was restricted to those who paid six *livres* in poll tax, the franchise was again practically universal. All persons aged twenty-five and over, whose names were inscribed on the taxation rolls, were eligible to vote either in the rural parochial assemblies or in urban guild assemblies. In the country districts, the elections of representatives of the third estate were conducted in two, in the towns in three or four stages, depending on whether the constituency was a primary or secondary bailliwick.

Partly because of this process of indirect election and partly because of the high level of illiteracy among the rural population, the representatives of the third estate in the States General were practically confined to the middle class. Although peasants vastly outnumbered townsmen in the composite electoral assemblies of the bailliwicks, peasant delegates were nearly always eliminated in the last stage of the election. In general, the representatives of the third estate consisted of experienced professional men of established reputation, among whom lawyers, as Burke noted, preponderated. For the most part the electors chose their delegates from members of the third estate—though there were notable exceptions. Both the abbé Sieyès and count de Mirabeau were elected for the third estate, although belonging respectively to the first and second orders. The clergy generally elected as its representatives humble parish priests (*curés*), only forty-six, out of the total ecclesiastical delegation of 300, being prelates. Few members of the Court aristocracy—an exception being the duke of Orléans—were chosen to represent the nobility. The majority of the second order consisted of materialistic and conservative provincial nobility, whose instructions left them little latitude to offer concessions to the third estate. There was, however, a strong contingent, about ninety in all, of the liberal aristocracy, this group being particularly prominent in the delegation from the capital. The total effective membership of the assembly amounted to 1,201 representatives, of whom 291 were lay nobles and 610 members of the third estate.

For the most part, the deputies elected were those who had been chiefly responsible for the drawing up of the lists of grievances or *cahiers* *de doléances*. Necker, in fact, made no effort to influence the elections, or to support official candidates. The same could not be said, however, of wealthy and powerful individuals, such as the duke of Orléans, who gave a lead to public opinion by the circulation of so-called 'model' *cahiers*, containing specimen lists of political and social reforms. Each order drew up its own *cahiers* at each stage of the electoral process. The *cahiers* which were actually taken to the States General by the deputies were those formulated in the electoral assemblies of the bailliwicks. It was at this stage that middle-class influence was brought to bear upon the demands which had been expressed in the *cahiers* of the primary assemblies of the third estate. The editing which then took place resulted, in many cases, in the elimination from the general *cahiers* of the characteristic social and economic demands of the rural proletariat. This procedure helps to explain why the grievances of the peasants were not ventilated in the national assembly and why nothing was done to dismantle the social framework of the *ancien régime* until the rural population revolted in the summer of 1789.

A comparison of the general *cahiers* of the various estates reveals a surprising measure of agreement on the most urgent tasks of reform, but a sharp divergence of view as to the political and social status to be accorded to the privileged orders. There was unanimity between the orders on the necessity of destroying royal and ministerial 'despotism', on the desirability of establishing individual liberty and liberty of the press. Privileged and unprivileged were also united in their demands for a constitution, for the control of taxation by periodical national assemblies, for a lightening of the burden of the indirect taxes, for the destruction of the internal customs barriers, and for a greater measure of effective decentralisation. On the other hand, it is clear, from an examination of the *cahiers* of the clergy and nobility, that the privileged classes were only prepared to sacrifice their fiscal immunities on definite conditions, and that they had not yet agreed to accept the principle of political equality with the third estate. The clergy were determined, if possible, to retain their corporate independence and the nobility to defend their traditional social distinctions, their feudal dues and their political control of the provincial estates. To that extent the *cahiers* reflect the political and social conflicts which divided France as the *ancien régime* drew to its close.

4

THE REVOLUTION OF THE LAWYERS
(5 MAY–27 JUNE 1789)

(i) *The opening of the States General*

The States General were formally opened by Louis XVI at Versailles
on 5 May 1789, the assembled delegates of the three orders in their
ceremonial dress taking their places in the great hall of the *Hôtel
des Menus Plaisirs*. On this occasion, the proceedings consisted of a
brief introductory speech by Louis, a formal address by Barentin
and a three-hour discourse by Necker. From the king's speech it
appeared that the government did not wish to restrict the States to
the consideration of purely fiscal problems, and Barentin explicitly
referred to the need for judicial and educational reform and for a
relaxation of the press censorship. The Keeper of the Seals, however,
roundly condemned what he was pleased to call 'the false and exaggerated maxims' of the pamphlet literature of the previous year,
and announced that the government would regard the principle of
voting by head as excluded unless it was freely approved by the
estates as a whole. Necker's speech, as was expected, was mainly
devoted to the financial problem. This he attributed to the credit
crisis consequent on the American war, and might well have been
solved, he suggested, without the summons of the States General.
The king's benevolence in a ssembling the delegates of the nation,
however, would rapidly rest ore public confidence and ensure budgetary equilibrium. On the crucial question of procedure, Necker
recommended that the Stat es should provisionally agree to the retention of voting by order, so as to allow the privileged classes voluntarily to resign their fiscal immunities, without being forced to do so
by the numerical preponderance of the third estate in common

sessions. Later, he suggested, the orders might negotiate the terms and conditions on which voting in common would prove acceptable to all parties. This solution was a moderate and sensible one, and might well have avoided the difficulties which were soon to divide the deputies. Though Necker did not refer to the need of periodical meetings of the States, and did not speak of the urgent task of framing a constitution, it would be untrue to say that he laid no positive programme of reforms before the assembly. He emphasised the need for the overhaul of taxation, both direct and indirect, for the abolition of the internal customs dues and of the oppressive salt tax. The minister also spoke of the possible extension to the whole kingdom of the system of provincial estates. This would have been a concession to the provincial nobility, and might have opened up the possibility of establishing a second chamber. Though the speech was well received, its defects as a programme of action were revealed once it had been printed. One clear-sighted foreign observer later summed up his impressions of the speech in the Churchillian phrase that 'never was so noble an opportunity more completely lost'.[1]

(ii) The conflict of the orders (6 May–9 June 1789)

In the absence of any firm lead from the government, the States were immediately plunged into unnecessary wrangles on the question of procedure. The *minutiae* and tiresomeness of their debates should not, however, deceive us as to the importance of the issues at stake, for the conflict ended in the assumption by the third estate of national sovereignty, in a humiliating defeat for the privileged orders, and open defiance of the king's authority. If we are to believe Dumont, 'all the seeds of disorder were sown and took root in this interval' and these procedural conflicts, therefore, deserve more notice than they are usually given by historians.[2]

On 5 May the assembly had been adjourned and nothing had been said about the separation of the orders for the transaction of business. Early next day, however, the deputies were informed by posters that 'the place set apart for their meeting would be ready to receive them by nine o'clock in the morning'. This announcement, too, seemed to imply the holding of common sessions, but it soon appeared that, by the king's authority, three separate chambers had been prepared. When the third estate reassembled in the *Salle des Menus*

1. *Groenvelt's Letters*, p. 17.
2. *Souvenirs sur Mirabeau et sur les deux premières Assemblées Legislatives*, ed. J. Bénétruy, Paris, 1951, p. 47. See also *Receuil de Documents relatifs aux Séances des Etats Généraux*. Edd. G. Lefebvre and A. Terroine. vol. I, 1953.

Plaisirs in order to check the election returns, they discovered that
the other two orders had met separately. In the course of the afternoon, news reached the third estate that the privileged orders intended
to verify their powers separately and that the nobility had adjourned
till 11 May. In this way arose a dispute between the orders on the
issue whether or not the powers of the deputies should be verified
in common. Behind this seemingly trifling issue, however, there
loomed the whole question of voting by head. If the first two orders
submitted to the verification of powers in common, it would be
difficult, if not impossible, for them to resist on the larger issue. If
voting in common were accepted as the normal method of procedure
it was clear that the double representation already granted to the
third estate would enable it to gain its way on all contentious issues
by sheer weight of voting strength in a single assembly.[1] On the
other hand, if the verification of powers were carried out separately
and the orders were constituted as separate chambers, it would be
just as difficult for the third estate to break down the traditional and
hitherto legal procedure of voting by order. The political ascendancy of the privileged orders would thus be assured and liberal
reform be dependent on the goodwill of the aristocracy.

In this struggle over the verification of powers the clergy occupied
a middle position between the two main contestants. Conscious of
its own internal divisions, and afraid of the consequences of popular
ill will if it sided with the nobility, the first order adopted a cautious
and temporising policy. This was apparent as early as 8 May for,
although the clergy verified its powers separately on that date, it
refrained from constituting itself as a separate chamber. Its next move
was to come forward as a mediator with the suggestion that the orders
should appoint commissioners to discuss their differences in a series
of conciliatory conferences. The numerical preponderance of the
parish priests and the liberal views of a group of powerful prelates
meant that, eventually, the clergy would support the third estate
rather than the nobility, at least on the question of the verification of
powers. That occurred, however, only after much discussion and many
heart-searchings, for the clergy were still reluctant to surrender
their corporate status. Here again fear entered into their calculations,
for they were uneasily aware that the confiscation of the church's
large landed estates as a possible solution for the country's financial
difficulties had already begun to be discussed.

1. Of 200 parish priests probably 125 would have voted with the third estate
together with at least fifty liberal nobles.

Although the nobility conducted its own case unskilfully, and in such a way as to ensure its final defeat, not all the arguments it employed in the dispute were without force. It is true that its appeal to traditional forms and historical precedents could not be expected to impress the third estate, but it was impossible to ignore the danger that the feudal dues, titles of nobility and other privileges might well be swept away without compensation, unless they could be initially debated on a basis of equality between the separate orders. It is easy to see, therefore, why the nobles regarded the separate verification of powers as the outer bastion of their whole defensive position. Moreover, many members of the liberal aristocracy, such as Lafayette, whose political sympathies lay with the third estate, were prevented by their binding instructions from their constituents, from openly supporting the principle of voting in common. When the nobility reassembled on 11 May it took up a position, from which it was difficult to recede, by immediately verifying its powers and constituting itself a separate chamber. Its agreement to take part in the conciliatory conferences held on 23 and 25 May implied no real change of heart. Discussions in these conferences therefore proved futile and, on 25 May, the meetings of commissioners were adjourned indefinitely. The nobility then threw down a direct challenge to the third estate by resolving, on 26 May, that it could not accept for the present session the common verification of powers and, on 28 May, that voting by order was a fundamental principle of the monarchical constitution. In this way, the nobility committed itself to a policy of no compromise.

Within the third estate, views as to possible solutions for the deadlock were divided, but there was no wavering on the question of principle. The attitude of the 'Commons' on the verification of powers was *prima facie* reasonable. To maintain that all the orders had a common interest in establishing the regularity of the election returns and that, therefore, this operation should be carried out in common session seemed only logical. The argument, however, that this procedure would not prejudice the right of the orders to sit and vote separately at a later stage was merely specious. And it soon became manifest that the Commons were seeking to raise and solve indirectly by this means the larger issue of voting by head. The third estate quickly shaped its tactics by determining, on 7 May, to entrench itself in its position by a stolid refusal either to verify its powers or to constitute itself as a separate chamber. These tactics, however, involved the Commons in makeshift arrangements for the regulation of their own proceedings, and frustrated the conciliatory moves made by Malouet on 6 and 15 May, with the object of removing the legitimate fears and anxieties of the privileged orders. Nevertheless, when the third estate discussed the clerical proposals for conciliatory conferences between 14 and 18 May, the moderate counsels of Rabaut de Saint-Étienne in favour of acceptance prevailed over the extremist views of Le Chapelier, who wished the assembly to reject them. After the failure of the negotiations and the hostile declaration of the nobility on 26 May, the Commons decided, largely on the advice of Mirabeau, to try and split the ranks of the privileged orders by winning over the clergy. An appeal to the clergy, drafted by the eminent lawyer Target, calling upon them 'in the name of the God of peace' to join the Commons in the hall of the general assembly, and to explore ways and means of breaking the deadlock, evoked so much sympathy among the parish priests on 27 May that only skilful delaying tactics on the part of the conservative bishops prevented the clergy from responding to the invitation.

On 28 May the government intervened to propose the resumption of the conciliatory conferences, this time in the presence of the royal ministers. This move, however, was regarded by the third estate, with some justification, as pointless in view of the uncompromising stand of the nobility. The government's motives were also suspect, since its intervention was obviously timed to prevent the threatened desertion of the clergy to the Commons. The ministerial conferences, held between 30 May and 9 June, were in fact as fruitless as the earlier discussions, for the nobility wrecked the proceedings by quarrelling on points of detail. In order to avert the threatened breakdown, Necker once more intervened, on 4 June, with a fresh proposal. He suggested that the powers of deputies whose election seemed *prima facie* in order, should be verified by the separate estates; that contested elections should be subject to joint examination by commissioners of the orders specifically appointed for the purpose. Where the recommendations of the joint commissioners proved unacceptable, a final verdict was to be given by the king. This mediation so obviously facilitated the maintenance of the separate orders that it seriously embarrassed the third estate. If it refused to discuss the proposal outright, it might find itself confronted with an alliance between the privileged orders and the Crown. Using the pretext, however, that the ministerial conferences had not yet been concluded, the Commons postponed their answer. Shortly afterwards, the nobility accepted the government's plan with so many reservations that it was easy for the Commons to contend that the privileged orders had virtually rejected the scheme.

(iii) *The formation of the National Assembly (10–17 June)*

The decisive moment in the long conflict between the orders was reached on 10 June. The third estate then invited the privileged orders, on the motion of the abbé Sieyès, to a common verification of powers and warned them that the election returns would be checked in the course of the day, whether the first two orders were present or not. This was a clear indication that the Commons were intent on proceeding to business and that they would refuse to recognise any deputies who did not submit to the common verification of their powers. Though the original motion had been redrafted to suit the moderates and had been coupled with the proposal that an address to the king should be made explaining why Necker's overture had been rejected, the Commons had now, in Sieyès' phrase, 'cut the cable'. The king's authority had been flouted and the initiative had been recaptured by the Commons.

On the evening of 12 June the Commons proceeded to call over the names and verify the powers of all the deputies, beginning with the privileged orders. This procedure was completed on 14 June, by which time the only members of the privileged classes who had joined the third estate were a few members of the lower clergy. After electing a president (Bailly) and two secretaries, the Commons then considered under what title it would constitute itself. Various alternatives were discussed but, with the exception of Mirabeau's suggestion of the 'representatives of the French people', these were all circumlocutions which could hardly have come into familiar use, even among the members themselves, and would certainly have been unintelligible to the general public. They were all more remarkable for forensic or philosophical subtlety than for common sense. When, however, on 16 June an obscure deputy from Berry named Legrand, probably prompted by Sieyès, proposed the title of 'National Assembly', there were dangerous signs of a schism in the Assembly. Late at night, the opponents of the motion withdrew from the Assembly and the president thought it wise to adjourn till next day. The motion was reformulated by Sieyès on 17 June and eventually carried by 490 votes to ninety. The resolutions and decrees of 17 June 1789 are important because they marked the assumption by the third estate of national sovereignty. Hitherto the Assembly had only come

to 'resolutions', now, for the first time, it passed 'decrees' and arro-
gated to itself, without the sanction of the Crown, the right to recast
the constitution.[1] The identification of the third estate with the nation
and the claim to the constituent power implied not only the disappearance of the distinction between the orders, formally abolished
on 5 November 1789, but also the abolition of the imperative mandates, which had so far acted as a restraining influence upon the
action of the representatives.[2] In self-defence against the anticipated
counter-move by the Crown, the Assembly also decreed, on the
motion of Le Chapelier, that the collection of the existing taxes, now
provisionally sanctioned, should cease, if for any reason it were
dissolved. A further decree provided that, as soon as the principles
of the constitution had been determined, the public debt should be
consolidated and given the guarantee of the French nation. In this
way it was hoped to dispose of the fears of national bankruptcy.

In passing these revolutionary decrees, the Assembly was well
aware of the dangers it was running, estimating correctly that the
court and the privileged orders would stop at nothing to overturn
them. It had, however, not acted rashly—for it had the support of
Paris and was calculating on being joined shortly by a majority
among the clergy and a minority among the nobles. So soon as that
happened, its claim to the title of National Assembly would be
unchallengeable. In fact, by a very narrow majority, the clergy voted
in favour of throwing in its lot with the third estate on 19 June.[3]

(iv) *The failure of counter-revolution (18–27 June)*

Meanwhile, during the temporary seclusion of the court at Marly,
owing to the death of the young Dauphin on 4 June, the representatives of reaction had brought their influence to bear on the king.
Powerful courtiers, headed by Louis XVI's younger brother, the

1. The claim to remodel the constitution was driven home on 9 July when the
Assembly took the new title of 'Constituent Assembly'.
2. The imperative mandates were abolished on 19 November 1789. Ever since then,
as Clemenceau noted, the French deputy has always been the representative, not of a
particular constituency, but of the nation.
3. Originally the votes cast in favour of the common verification of powers had
totalled only 127 as against 136 for separate verification, while ten of the clergy had
voted for common verification provided that it did not prejudice the distinction between the orders. After failing to convert the ten to their point of view, the minority
decided to adopt the proviso, with the result that a majority of one was obtained. After
a violent protest the president of the clerical order left the chamber followed by his
supporters, and when a fresh vote was taken, with the bishop of Vienne in the chair,
it was found that there was a majority of twelve in favour of common verification—
on the condition mentioned above.

count d'Artois, had urged the sovereign to take a firm stand against
the revolutionary claims of the third estate. The presidents of the
privileged orders in the States General—the cardinal de la Roche-
foucauld and the duke de Montmorency-Luxembourg—insisted
that the monarch, in his own interest, should make common cause
with the nobility. D'Espréménil, once the foremost assailant of
monarchical despotism, and now a prominent advocate of reaction,
persuaded the *parlement* of Paris to send secret deputations to the
king to recommend the forcible dissolution of the National Assembly.
Louis was now faced with a dilemma: if he supported the nobility,
he might well identify the monarch with a lost cause; if, on the other
hand, he sanctioned the decrees of 17 June, he would alienate the
privileged orders and also involve himself in a humiliating submission to the radical extremists in the assembly.

In this situation Louis was easily persuaded by Necker that the
time had arrived for the royal mediation to be imposed on the
contending parties in the Assembly. Taken unawares by the decrees
of 17 June, the minister had decided that it was now imperative,
before the situation became worse, for the king to vindicate his
sovereign authority by terminating the conflict between the orders
and by taking the initiative in legislative reform. Such action might
well bring the hotheads in both camps to their senses; it might also
help to re-establish the minister's waning prestige in the royal council
and to rescue the king from his dilemma. If the verification of powers
in common could be brought about, not as the result of a decree of
the National Assembly, but in obedience to the royal command,
appearances might yet be saved. To allow the conflict to continue
would only make civil war inevitable.

Such were the arguments used by Necker to support his recommendation that a royal session (*séance royale*) should be held without
delay in the States General. The suggestion was based upon an
accurate appreciation of the existing situation and of the balance of
the opposing forces. It was consistent with the policy which Necker
had advocated since the meeting of the Assembly and the scheme,
as originally conceived, would have involved real concessions to the
third estate. The programme of reforms which Louis was asked to
sponsor would have converted the king, in effect, into a limited
constitutional monarch. It remained to be seen, however, whether
Necker could persuade the royal council, since increasing pressure
was now being exerted on the king by the reactionary party. The
minister's draft proposals were initially submitted to a meeting

of the council held at Marly on 19 June. On this occasion, the normal membership of the *Conseil des dépêches* was increased by the presence of four Councillors of State, who formed the special commission established by Barentin to deal with the affairs of the States General. Necker attempted to steer a middle course between the contestants by classifying the subjects for discussion in the States General into two categories—those to be decided in common sessions and those reserved for separate discussion by the orders meeting independently. In essence, his solution was to include in the latter category matters involving the vested interests of the individual estates, but to include among the subjects for common discussion the question of the future constitution of the States General. Discussion in the council on this and other points was acrimonious, but the vital decision was taken to hold a royal session on 22 June. Orders were given to the Grand Master of Ceremonies to make the necessary preparations and to close the main assembly hall used by the deputies of the third estate.

When the president of the National Assembly, Bailly, and his colleagues attempted to resume their proceedings on the morning of 20 June, they found the hall closed against them. Indignation ran high and the deputies drew the conclusion that the government had decided to dissolve the States General in order to prevent the Commons from being joined by the majority of the clergy. Some of the members wished to transfer their meetings to Marly, so as to be able to obstruct the intrigues of the reactionary groups surrounding the king. Others, such as Sieyès, advocated that the representatives should resort to Paris, where they would be under the protection of the mob. Finally, on the motion of Dr Guillotin, the deputies reassembled in an adjoining tennis court. Here it was resolved by acclamation that the members of the National Assembly should take a solemn oath, to be confirmed by their signatures, not to separate until the constitution had been established on firm foundations. After Bailly and the two secretaries had sworn first, this pledge was taken by all the deputies, with the single exception of Martin Dauch of Castelnaudary. This celebrated oath was historically significant as the first act of formal disobedience to the king and also because it was subscribed even by those deputies who had opposed the decrees of 17 June. The oath had been suggested by Mounier, seconded and drafted by Target, Barnave and Le Chapelier. All were members of the legal profession.

While these proceedings were drawing to a close, the council had reassembled at Marly to resume its discussions on Necker's proposals for the royal session. According to Necker's own account, the council agreed to approve his plans with minor modifications and was preparing to break up, when the king was summoned from the council chamber by the queen. As a result of the queen's intervention, so Necker's version continues, the debate was re-opened, final approval was withheld and the royal session was postponed from 22 June to the following day. This account probably errs in attributing too great a share of the responsibility for this fateful decision to Marie Antoinette. According to Barentin, no decision had been reached when the king was called from the meeting, since Necker's proposals had been subjected from the outset to severe and hostile criticism. This seems inherently more probable.

On 21 June the court returned to Versailles and the next council meeting, held the same day, was attended by the king's brothers, Provence and Artois. By that time, the opposition to Necker's programme of liberal reforms had hardened and the financier found that he could only rely on the support of Montmorin, the Foreign Minister. It was thus that the struggle inside the council between Necker and Barentin was resolved in favour of the latter. It was finally decided to quash the decrees of 17 June, to make the future organisation of the States subject to discussion by the separate orders, and to overawe the Commons by a display of armed force. The preparations for the royal session were now complete, but its chances of success had already been compromised, firstly by its postponement till 23 June and, secondly, by Necker's decision to absent himself from the ceremony. The postponement gave the majority of the clergy the opportunity to join forces with the third estate in the nave of the church of St Louis on 22 June. Necker's action in dissociating himself from the proceedings stigmatised the royal session as an attempt at counter-revolution.

On Tuesday, 23 June, Louis XVI, when communicating the council's decisions to the deputies, was surrounded for the last time with the full panoply of royal majesty. The royal session at which the king appeared in person to announce his solution of the vexed constitutional problems and to declare his legislative intentions, bore the character partly of a *lit de justice* and partly of a military *coup de force*. The tenseness of the situation in Versailles and Paris, the solemnity of the proceedings in the States General and the magnitude of the issues at stake, marked the occasion as a crisis in the relations of the monarchy and the National Assembly. Later events were to show that it was also a turning-point in the history of the revolution.

Nothing had been neglected to prevent outbursts of popular sympathy with the deputies. Four thousand troops had been concentrated in Versailles and six regiments posted in the outskirts. The assembly hall had been cleared of spectators and the Master of Ceremonies had even seen fit to keep the third estate waiting in the rain outside, while the privileged orders were allowed to take their places undisturbed. At noon, the king left the royal palace amid fanfares of trumpets and the rolling of drums, accompanied by his household guards and cavalry. According to one eye-witness of the scene, 'Louis affected to smile, but it was with an ill grace. The ironical gaiety of the count d'Artois appeared much more natural; he had the air of one riding in triumph, and leading the king bound as his captive'. Although the customary cries of 'Long live the King' were raised as the cavalcade passed on its way to the assembly, and although Louis was greeted, on his arrival, with acclamations from the nobility and clergy he was received by the rest of the assembly in complete silence.

Louis opened the session with a short speech in which he referred to the conflicts dividing the estates. In effect, he appealed to the members of the first two orders to set an example of reconciliation and compromise. Barentin then read a royal declaration outlining the procedure to be followed in the current sessions of the States General.[1] The decrees of 17 June and the subsequent resolutions of the National Assembly were declared null and void. The sanctity of the ancient distinction between the estates was re-affirmed. The king recommended, but did not impose, the acceptance by the orders of the principle of common sessions in matters of common concern. He explicitly reserved, however, for separate deliberation by the estates the ancient rights, feudal and titular prerogatives of the first two orders, ecclesiastical discipline and, above all, the constitutional forms of future States General. In order to remove all obstacles in the way of such separate sessions, the king also released the the deputies from the binding instructions of their constituents. The procedure recommended by Necker on 4 June for the determination of disputed election returns was now enforced. And, finally, the king expressly forbade the estates, either when assembled in com-

---

1. Before 1789 royal 'declarations' were generally employed to alter or modify existing arrangements resulting either from custom of from previous edicts and ordinances.

mon or in their separate chambers, to allow any strangers to attend their debates.[1]

A second royal declaration was then read summarising the legislative programme which Louis had approved. No loans were to be raised, no new taxes established or old ones prolonged without the consent of the States General. A return of state revenue and expenditure was to be published annually and the sums appropriated to the various departments were to be fixed and unalterable. This seemed to be a tardy recognition of the strict system of financial control which had been demanded by the assembly of Notables in 1787. Some direct taxes, such as the *taille*, some state and feudal obligations such as the *corvée*, were to be abolished outright, while the salt tax and the excise duties were to be reformed. In place of the provincial assemblies set up in 1787 the government proposed to extend to the whole kingdom the system of provincial estates. Although the constitution of these bodies was to be altered by the concession of double representation for the third estate, the change in the system of local government was, in effect, designed in the interests of the nobility. With suitable safeguards, the system of arbitrary arrest and imprisonment, of militia service and of press censorship were to be dispensed with. The task of reforming civil and criminal justice was to be resumed, the internal customs barriers removed and the administration of the royal domain reorganised.

Embedded among these blue-prints of reform, however, were articles which made it clear that the social fabric of the *ancien régime* was to be preserved intact. The king categorically declared that ecclesiastical tithes, feudal and manorial dues were to be treated as proprietary rights and, therefore, held sacred. The furthest the king would go to break down feudal privilege was a promise to sanction the surrender of the fiscal immunities of the privileged orders, but only if the sacrifice was made voluntarily. The culminating note of royal authority was struck in a final speech by the king, in which a scarcely veiled threat of dissolution was made, if the states did not submit to these regulations. Louis then ordered the estates to resume their discussions on the following day in the separate chambers which had been assigned to them.

When the king left the assembly, followed obediently by the main body of the privileged orders, it remained to be seen whether

1. Hitherto, the Commons had been alone in admitting spectators to their debates and the presence of observers in the third estate had done a great deal to encourage the radical elements in the Assembly.

the third estate would submit. This was put to the test when the
Grand Master of Ceremonies, the marquis de Brezé, reappeared
and called on the remaining deputies to break off their proceedings
in accordance with the king's instructions. Bailly, as president, replied that, although the Assembly stood adjourned, it could not be
dismissed until it had debated the matter. It was at this point that
Mirabeau rose in his place and delivered the apostrophe to de Brezé
which made the occasion historic.

'Sir, you are a stranger in this assembly, you have not the right to speak
here: if the King wishes to communicate his intentions to us, he can do
so through the Keeper of the Seals; in any case, we shall not leave;
return to those who have sent you and tell them that we shall not stir
from our places save at the point of the bayonet.'[1]

After this dramatic intervention, which reaffirmed its determination
to implement the Tennis Court Oath, the assembly proceeded to
confirm the decrees of 17 June and to proclaim the freedom of its
members from arrest. The passive resistance of the deputies did not,
however, suffice to defeat the contemplated counter-revolution.
Soon after his return to the palace, Louis gave orders for the dissolution of the estates and these would have been carried out by his
bodyguards, but for a further stand in defence of the Commons by a
group of liberal nobles. The rest of the day was chiefly remarkable
for noisy popular demonstrations in sympathy with Necker, whose
proffered resignation the court felt it inexpedient for the moment to
accept.

The king's decision not to push the issue to the point of civil war
did not, however, weaken the determination of the privileged orders.
On 25 June the clergy at last formally constituted itself and, together
with the nobility, adhered to the royal declarations made during the
royal session. During the next two days, only twenty-one further
members of the clergy and fifty nobles deserted to the third estate.
This schism was a direct result of mob intimidation and was facilitated by the understanding that verification in common would not
prejudice the maintenance of the orders. The situation on the morning
of 27 June was thus that the States General were divided into two
groups—830 representatives of the nation and 371 representatives

1. The exact words used by Mirabeau cannot now be established but the above
quotation is probably fairly accurate. The Master of Ceremonies had, in fact, only
the right of delivering written, and not verbal, messages from the king.

of the privileged orders. It seems certain that the resistance of the latter would have been prolonged, but for the royal orders issued during the day commanding the privileged classes to fuse with the third estate. That surrender too had been provoked by fear. Louis had during the morning received news from Paris that, unless the fusion of the orders was prescribed by royal authority, a mob of 30,000 would enforce the decision by invading the palace. In other words, the pacific revolution of the lawyers had only been consummated by the threat from Paris of the intervention of the mob.

One or two comments may be made on the course of events since the opening of the States General. The first is that the programme of liberal reforms and the method of procedure proclaimed at the royal session should have been announced on 5 May, at a time when the third estate was expecting a lead from the government, and when the privileged orders were hoping that their material interests would be protected from the consequences of the grant of double representation for the Commons. Before passions on both sides had been enflamed by the conflict over procedure an authoritative royal declaration would have stood a good chance of acceptance and the transition to limited monarchy might have been achieved without resort to counter-revolution on the one hand or appeal to mass violence on the other. By 23 June, however, such a solution had ceased to be practical politics. Secondly, there can be little doubt that the weak and vacillating character of Louis XVI was chiefly to blame for the discredit in which the monarchy was involved by its association with counter-revolutionary intrigue and its subsequent surrender to the unilateral decisions of the National Assembly. A stronger king would not have subjected the fate of the monarchy to the contradictory advice of rival politicians and would have seized the chance of mediating between the orders. Louis' lethargic and easy-going nature, his lack of independent judgement and his inability to grasp the seriousness of his situation until it was too late, his subservience to his wife and his irresolution caused him to adopt a policy of sheer inaction, the consequences of which were disastrous.

The wisdom of Necker's policy after 17 June is difficult to judge, for the evidence which would enable us to compare his original drafts of the royal declarations for the royal session with the final version has been destroyed. The suggestion of a royal session was not, in itself, unstatesmanlike. Mirabeau later expressed the view that if the substance of the royal reforms had been conveyed to the assembly in a more conciliatory fashion, instead of through a medium recalling the most arbitrary features of a *lit de justice*, the kingdom would have been at Louis' feet. It was not the conception, but rather the execution of the *séance royale*, which had been at fault. This does not, however, clear Necker of all blame. Even if Barentin had not turned the issues of policy into a personal vendetta by conspiring against Necker in the interests of counter-revolution, it is doubtful whether the dispositions made for the royal session would have been substantially different. Though Necker was able, by staying away from the ceremony, to outwit his opponents, it is significant that, when he withdrew his resignation, he made no attempt to displace Barentin or to insist on a change of policy. After 23 June Barentin and his followers still retained the conviction that victory could yet be theirs if resort were had, not to legal forms, which lawyers could resist, but to military force. Perhaps Mirabeau could be taken at his word and an appeal made to the bayonet. Such a move assumed that the monarchy could rely on its own troops, which, as events were to prove, was now doubtful.[1]

1. For the constitutional struggles in the Estates General see *Receuil de Documents relatifs aux Séances des Etats Généraux* (*Mai–Juin, 1789*), edited under the direction of G. Lefebvre, 2 vols., Paris, 1953–1962.

5

THE REVOLT OF THE MASSES AND
THE FALL OF THE 'ANCIEN REGIME'

(i) *The revolt of Paris and the fall of the Bastille*

Though Necker continued in office after 23 June, his influence in the government declined sharply, and royal policy was henceforth shaped by Barentin and the court reactionaries. Preparations were hastily made for a *coup de force*. On 26 June six regiments were ordered up to Versailles and on 1 July ten other regiments, mostly of Germans and Swiss, were called in from the provinces to throw a cordon round the capital. These troops were timed to arrive between 5 and 10 July. Marshal de Broglie was placed in supreme command at Versailles, while Besenval, a Swiss, acting under Broglie's orders, was given the responsible task of effecting the concentrations round Paris. It was soon rumoured that the purpose of these dispositions was to enable the reactionaries to reverse the victory won by the National Assembly on 23 June, and to enforce the policy enunciated at the Royal Session. Substance was given to these popular suspicions when, on 2 and 3 July, the former presidents of the clergy and nobility reaffirmed the right of the privileged orders to hold separate sessions. Shortly afterwards the aristocratic delegates who had submitted unwillingly to the royal orders to join the third estate on 27 June, absented themselves from the debates in the assembly, or ostentatiously refrained from voting. Measures were also taken to restore discipline among the troops at Versailles by confining in the Abbaye prison at Paris members of the French guards, who had displayed their sympathy with the popular cause on the occasion of the Royal Session.

On 8 July, when the troop concentrations had already begun,

Mirabeau voiced the anxiety of the Assembly at the turn of events, and it was decided to petition the king to countermand his orders. The royal reply, on 10 July, merely referred to the necessity of preserving order in the capital and of protecting the assembly itself, which it was suggested might well be transferred for greater safety to Noyon or Soissons. Street-rioting had, it is true, already attained serious proportions, for on 30 June, the French guards imprisoned at the Abbaye had been released by mobs assembled at the Palais Royal. Between 10 and 13 July evidence of the preparations for a general insurrection in the capital accumulated, when the customs surrounding Paris were systematically destroyed. This ring of customs barriers, which had been constructed by Calonne between 1784 and 1786, was one of the most hated institutions of the *ancien régime*. All meat, wines, vegetables, livestock and building materials entering Paris had, in this way, been subjected to heavy tolls which went to line the pockets of the farmers-general. The most active elements in the riots were apparently wine merchants and professional smugglers, but the mobs were, no doubt, convinced that, as a result of the demolitions, the prices of consumers' goods in the capital would fall. Subsequent investigations, however, proved that this extensive wrecking operation had been planned and controlled by leaders acting under instructions from the centre of Orléanist intrigue, the Palais Royal. Those who had directed the risings had been concerned, not merely to destroy the evil legacy of Calonne, but to facilitate the entry of food supplies and the collection of arms. The inhabitants of Paris obviously considered themselves as a beleaguered garrison, whose most pressing needs would be provisions and the means of self-defence.

Meanwhile, it had been decided at court that, if the royal declarations of 23 June were to be implemented, the existing ministry would need to be reconstructed. On 11 July, therefore, Necker had been dismissed and ordered to leave the country and, at the same time, his supporters in the council, Montmorin, St Priest and Puységur had also been relieved of their offices. The new administration, appointed the following day, included the Marshal de Broglie at the War Department, la Porte at the Admiralty, la Vauguyon at the Foreign Office and was headed by de Breteuil—a favourite of the queen and a notorious reactionary. The dismissal of Necker was generally interpreted to mean that the dissolution of the assembly and the repudiation of the public debt were imminent. In Paris, where the news of the ministerial changes was received on 12 July, consternation was general. Continuing troop movements raised the fears of the inhabitants to fever pitch. On 13 July disorders continued when rioters from the faubourg St Denis broke into and looted the monastery of St Lazare. This convent was unpopular because it was used as a prison and was also suspected of being a centre for the storage of grain and an arms depot. Armed mobs, once more directed from the Palais Royal, released the prisoners, removed large quantities of corn and flour to the central markets and carried out wholesale looting and pillaging. This incident is historically important because it convinced the existing municipal authorities of the necessity of taking immediate measures to protect life and property in the capital. It was decided that each of the six districts, into which Paris had been divided for the purpose of electing representatives to the States General, should form a contingent of 200 citizens capable of bearing arms to act as a militia under the control of a permanent committee at the Hôtel de Ville. This municipal guard was formed the same night, when the existing municipal authorities appointed by the king were fused with the members of the electoral assembly of Paris to form a new commune.

The storming and capture of the Bastille on 14 July is one of the best known and least understood events of the revolution. The object of the attackers was not the release of the prisoners, but the collection of arms. The actual assault of the fortress was the result of a misunderstanding, and its capture was the achievement, not of the mob, but of the French guards. This time there was little evidence that operations had been directed from the Palais Royal, for most of the so-called 'Conquerors of the Bastille', whose exploits became a popular legend, were small workshop masters and their journeymen assistants from the immediate locality of the faubourg St Antoine. Though the horrors of the Bastille as a state prison had been the theme of radical pamphleteers, such as Linguet, and of sentimental poets like Cowper, it had never been used as a place of confinement for the poor and its contemporary and subsequent repute as a symbol of monarchical and feudal tyranny was exaggerated. On 14 July 1789, the Bastille had a completely different significance for the people of Paris, who were hourly expecting the intervention of the foreign regiments surrounding the city. It was feared, not because it was a prison, but because it was an arms depot and a citadel, whose guns were menacing from their embrasures the eastern quarters of the capital. Earlier in the day, the Hôtel des Invalides had been ransacked for arms and a vain search made in the Carthusian

monastery. The mob which concentrated round the Bastille with the
same object did not originally intend to attack it, and, of their two
main demands, one at least, the withdrawal of the guns, was granted
by the governor, de Launay, before a shot was fired. The fortress
was short of supplies and poorly defended, and negotiations for its
surrender between the delegates of the electoral assembly of Paris
and the governor might well have been successful, but for a misunderstanding. De Launay had promised not to fire upon the crowd
while the negotiations were proceeding, unless the fortress was
attacked. Two men, however, managed to climb into one of the inner
courts and to break the chains of the drawbridge, thus allowing the
mob to gain entrance. The governor appears to have lost his nerve
and the garrison fired. The crowd, thinking that the drawbridge had
been lowered by the defenders and suspecting a trap, then began
to attack the fortress. A further volley from the garrison, while
attempts were being made by delegates from the Hôtel de Ville to
arrange a parley, strengthened the impression of treachery. Three
hundred French guards were despatched by the municipal authorities
and cannon taken from the Invalides were now employed against
the fortress. This induced de Launay to make a formal offer of
capitulation, but the mob was determined that the Bastille should
be taken by storm. When the fortress eventually fell, its governor
was massacred by the crowd in front of the town hall, and de
Flesselles, the official head of the former municipal authority, who
was thought to have misdirected the rioters in their search for arms,
shared the same fate.

No other single event in the revolution had so many-sided or
far-reaching results as the fall of the Bastille. It marked the end of
royal despotism in France, completed the transfer of political
authority to the national legislature, and by encouraging the peasants
to revolt, paved the way for the fall of feudalism. It freed the country
from the restraints of press censorship and thus led to the rise of
popular journalism, the political effect of which was amply demonstrated in the preparation of the next revolutionary *journée* in the
following October. It was accompanied by an important revolution
in the municipal administration of Paris and was quickly followed
by an almost complete decentralisation of government. It provoked
the first emigration of the reactionary nobility, led by the count
d'Artois, and set in train the forces that led, in time, to foreign
intervention and war with Europe. For the moment, however, the
impression made by the news from Paris in foreign countries was

wholly favourable. The popular vengeance taken on de Launay and de Flesselles was condoned, the heroism of the mob loudly proclaimed and the absence of any private plundering generally admired. The fall of the fortress was widely acclaimed as heralding a new birth of liberty, not only in France, but throughout the world.

The immediate effects of 14 July were the resignation of Breteuil's ministry, the recall of Necker, the withdrawal of the military forces surrounding the capital, the election of Bailly as mayor of Paris and of Lafayette as commander of the newly organised National Guard. The personal visit of Louis XVI to the capital on 17 July, the adoption of the tricolour as the national flag and the formation of the new municipality or Commune gave formal recognition to the victory of the people of Paris.[1] The Chief beneficiaries, however, were the members of the National Assembly, who were not only freed from the danger of dissolution, but were vested with fresh powers to proceed with the work of constitution-making and liberal reform. The minority of the clergy and nobility who had joined the third estate on 27 June with reservations and protests now surrendered their scruples and abandoned the struggle to maintain their separate corporate existence. The proud magistrates of the *parlement* of Paris, who had so recently encouraged the court in the attempt at counter-revolution, appeared before the National Assembly with lowly submission and acknowledged its sovereign authority.

(ii) *The revolt of the provinces and the 'Great Fear'*

The revolt of the capital and the formation of the new Commune also produced immediate and widespread repercussions in the provinces. Open dissatisfaction with the oligarchical composition of their municipal corporations had already been shown in the spring of 1789 by the townsmen and villagers. The news of the fall of the Bastille caused this discontent in the second half of July to assume a new pitch of intensity. The municipal revolts, which then spread across France, assumed, in general, three forms. In some areas, a formal and peaceful transformation occurred, the town corporations agreeing to adopt the national cockade and to broaden the basis of their authority. In other districts, notably at Rouen, Lyons and Dijon, the transition to the new régime assumed a more radical form. Special committees were established to deal with the rising food scarcities and permanent committees were organised to control the

1. The tricolour was formed from the red and blue colours of the city of Paris, and the white emblem of the Bourbons.

new municipal militias. As in the capital, these militias were designed, on the one hand, to afford protection against the danger of
counter-revolution and, on the other, to check the excesses of
popular violence. In yet other areas, the failure of local rioters to
obtain the satisfaction of their demands for the control of food
prices led them forcibly to expel the municipal corporations and to
pillage the houses of local grain merchants. In such cases, new and
more democratic municipal institutions were brought into existence
forthwith. In these troubles and disturbances the authority and
control hitherto exercised by the central power over local administration collapsed. The *intendants* were either expelled or themselves
recognised the impossibility of continuing in office. As will be seen
later, this *de facto* displacement of municipal authority made effective
decentralisation in France a foregone conclusion.

In the spring of 1789 France had also been convulsed by a series
of widespread agrarian revolts. The peasants, who formed about
70 per cent of the country's population, had eagerly anticipated
that the meeting of the States General would bring about the
speedy abolition of their state and feudal burdens. The apparent
inactivity of the National Assembly and its failure to consider
agrarian problems had profoundly disillusioned the rural inhabitants.
The latter were also experiencing the full and disastrous effects of the
bad harvest of 1788. Bread prices in the country districts were half
as high again as in the capital and in the towns, where prices were, to
some extent, controlled by means of Government subsidies. In these
circumstances peasant consumers had crowded into the local town
markets, hoping to avail themselves of the supplies requisitioned by
the municipal authorities and disposed of at below cost price. Here
they had come into contact with the municipal revolts and had thus
learned a lesson in the effectiveness of violent protests. The peasants,
however, had been mainly provoked by the increasing burden, in
famine conditions, of their feudal payments in kind. These not only
reduced still further the scanty grain stocks available, but also increased the monetary income of their feudal superiors, as prices
rocketed. Agrarian revolts and local *jacqueries* had, therefore, spread
widely. Enclosures had been broken down, common land reoccupied,
tithes and feudal dues refused and manorial records destroyed by the
burning of *châteaux*.

These peasant revolts were intensified in the latter part of July and
early August by the phenomenon of mass hysteria known as the
'Great Fear'. This may be described as a series of chain reactions to

local rumours of the approach of 'brigands' in the pay of the aristocrats. Of the reality of counter-revolutionary activity at Versailles there could be no doubt and the existence of large bodies of unemployed mendicants gave further support to the rumours. Here again the influence of the Parisian rising was felt, for the dispersal to the country districts of the military forces surrounding the capital was interpreted by the ignorant peasants as an incursion of armed bandits. The formation of the National Guard in Paris also gave rise to the supposition that the large floating population of unemployed ne'er-do-wells in the capital would shortly descend upon the countryside. The expeditions sent from the towns to requisition corn, and the convoys organised for the protection of supplies on the way to the town markets did nothing to dispel the scares. Even the defeat of counter revolution in Paris contributed to unnerve the peasants who assumed that the aristocrats would suborn escaped prisoners, unemployed vagabonds and even foreign mercenaries in a desperate attempt to recapture their control over events. The flight of the *émigrés* of 14 July was, therefore, regarded as a preliminary to their return supported by bands of Sardinian or Spanish brigands. The lack of any provincial newspaper press, the misguided efforts of local magistrates and clergy to warn their neighbours of the approach of suspected 'brigands', and the general assumption that those who were sceptical were themselves in league with the reactionaries helped to propagate the local scares and to spread consternation and anxiety. No less than six separate scares seem to have been started by purely local incidents, but the current of alarm and suspicion thus generated soon involved whole provinces. In this way, a local panic originating in Franche Comté spread southwards down the valley of the Rhône to Provence, eastwards to the Alps and westwards to the central plateau. Another scare was carried from Ruffec, south of Poitiers, to the Pyrenees, north-eastwards as far as Berry and also the Auvergne. The only areas of the country which were free from these panics were Alsace, Lorraine and Brittany.

(iii) *The fall of the* ancien régime (*4–11 August 1789*)

From the point of view of the National Assembly, the essential difference between the municipal and agrarian revolts was that the former had been started by middle-class notables who had, in most cases, shown a proper regard for private property, whereas the latter had been provoked by a rural proletariat, which had turned against landed proprietors as well as its feudal superiors. If public order in

the provinces was to be restored and private property protected, it
seemed necessary, therefore, either to repress the agrarian outrages
outright, or to make some immediate and striking concessions.
The dispersal of the military forces of the Crown left the Assembly
with only the second alternative and, in any case, the support of the
peasants was just as indispensable to the middle-class representatives as that of the working class in the capital. Hitherto, the deputies,
taking as their guide the general *cahiers* of the bailliwicks, had
concentrated on the task of formulating the principles of the constitution. Events had now shown, however, that the grievances which
had been expressed in the parochial *cahiers* would need to take precedence. Logically, also, the decision taken on 4 August, to draw
up a Declaration of Rights, seemed to require the overthrow of feudal
privilege. The nobility, moreover, had seen the necessity of bending
to the storm, if some remnants of their proprietary rights were to
be saved.

The surrender of their feudal rights and fiscal immunities by the
aristocracy and clergy on the night of 4 August was not, therefore,
the product of spontaneous generosity. Fear, calculation and suspicion inspired the action of many deputies and the famous session
was a parliamentary manœuvre planned by a radical 'cave' in the
Breton club on the previous day. The plot was that the partial
surrender of feudal privileges should be proposed by members of the
liberal nobility at an evening meeting, at which, it was hoped, opponents of the measure would not be present. The initiative was left to
the duke d'Aiguillon, whose example as one of the largest landed
proprietors in the country would, it was thought, sway the attitude
of the more conservative provincial nobility. In fact, d'Aiguillon's
motion was anticipated by the viscount de Noailles, who proposed
that the Assembly should decree complete fiscal equality and the
redemption of all feudal dues, except those involving personal
servitude. The latter, he suggested, should be abolished outright. This
motion, and not d'Aiguillon's, passed the Assembly and set the
tone of the unprecedented sacrifices which followed. In a mounting
spirit of patriotic enthusiasm the representatives of privilege came
forward to propose the admission of all citizens to public office
and the abolition of feudal jurisdictions, exclusive hunting rights
and the purchase of judicial and other offices. Even more impressive
and dramatic according to Dumont, who was an eye-witness of the
scene, was the surrender of all municipal, corporate and provincial
privileges, proposed by the representatives from Dauphiné. The

proceedings closed with a loyal address to the king, conferring on him the title of 'Restorer of French liberty'.

In their enthusiasm, however, the members of the National Assembly had overshot the mark, and cooler reflection on the part of the nobility prompted them later to restrict and even to contest some of these sacrifices. The result was that, when the decisions of principle were cast in legislative form between 5 and 11 August, middle-class conservatism and legal caution preserved many features of the fedual régime, which had been over-hastily condemned on the night of 4 August. In this way, the 'St Bartholomew of privilege' came to be a misnomer. Though the *ancien régime* had been dismantled, the declaration of the Assembly that 'the feudal régime had been entirely destroyed' was misleading. In the final draft, ecclesiastical tithes were abolished, but the most onerous of the feudal dues—those of a contractual nature—were made subject to redemption. Until they were redeemed, on terms which were left for settlement at a later stage, they were to be levied as before. The disillusionment of the peasants was complete and when the king refused his sanction to this limited social revolution the Assembly found itself in a quandary.

(iv) *The Declaration of Rights* (*26 August 1789*)

Between 12 and 26 August the Assembly resumed the discussion of a Declaration of Rights, which had been interrupted by the disturbing news from the provinces. The formulation of such a declaration had been demanded in the general *cahiers* and the discussion of draft proposals had begun after the re-election of a constitutional committee on 14 July. This committee proposed, on 28 July, that a text of the declaration should be agreed before the Assembly proceeded to frame a constitution. The decision to do so was taken on 4 August, under the stimulus of the provincial revolts. Some of the moderates, however, including Malouet and Mirabeau, argued that such a move would be unwise. They feared that a declaration would encourage discontented elements to enforce their rights or claims by continued violence. If the natural rights of men were first enunciated and then restricted in the constitution, the contradiction would, they contended, dismay and antagonise those whose expectations had thereby been falsified. Alternatively, if this danger was borne in mind, the Assembly would be obliged to be so cautious in the statement of political principles that the declaration would be false and lacking in general appeal. Barnave and Duport, however, rejected

with contempt the argument that the people should be kept in
ignorance of their rights lest they should abuse them. On the contrary, they felt that it would be essential, in view of the continuing
danger of counter-revolution, to register the early political conquests of the revolution in a solemn declaration, which would formally attest the demise of the *ancien régime*. Since the whole object of
the establishment of a constitution was to preserve the natural
rights of man, it ought to be prefaced by a declaration of what those
rights were. Such a statement, Barnave urged, would be a 'national
catechism', which would provide a standard by which the constitution could be judged and would, as Talleyrand emphasised, afford
a guide for those who framed it. Mounier contended that the declaration would be a statement, not of political rights, on which the
people could rest impossible claims, but of natural rights, which
were eternal, inalienable and imprescriptible. Finally, it was said that
the example of the English and American declarations should not
only be imitated but improved upon and that, in this respect, France
owed a debt to mankind.

In its final form the historic declaration, completed on 26 August,
reflected the views of men like Lafayette, Mounier, Talleyrand,
Lally Tollendal and Alexandre de Lameth who contributed most of
the work of drafting. In its political clauses it propounded the senti-
ments of middle-class individualism, in its religious articles it
expressed those of the Gallican Church and, in social and economic
matters, its doctrines were derived directly from the Physiocrats.
Though its significance in world history rested on the universality of
its appeal, many of its most important clauses directly condemned
the wrongs under which Frenchmen had suffered under the *ancien
régime*. The declaration was not, therefore, a formulation of purely
abstract doctrines unrelated to the historical context, but, on the
contrary, was realistic and even negative in its approach to the political problems of the moment. It was precisely for that reason that the
deductive and metaphysical draft prepared by Sieyès was rejected.

The two fundamental doctrines which gave the declaration its
force as the gospel of the revolution were those of natural rights and
national sovereignty. The natural rights of man and of the citizen,
stated in the preamble to be inalienable and sacred, were those derived
not from the existence of man in a state of nature, but from human
personality. Article II of the declaration defined these rights as
'liberty, property, security and the right to resist oppression'.
Two aspects of liberty—individual liberty and freedom of opinion—

were defined in more detail. Article VII, for example, declared that no man could be accused, arrested, or imprisoned except by due legal process, thus preventing the revival of *lettres de cachet*. Article VIII condemned punishment under retrospective legislation, while article IX, by adopting the principle of English law that all men are to be presumed innocent until they have been found guilty, excluded the use of torture. Freedom of speech, liberty of the press and toleration of the expression of religious opinions, were, with due and proper safeguards, conceded in articles X and XI. Nothing further was said to define the scope and implications of the other natural rights —except that property was described in article XVII as an 'inviolable and sacred right', and the right to compensation in case of expropriation was specifically enunciated. The latter provision was intended to ensure the redemption of the feudal dues, in accordance with the decrees of 4–11 August. The declaration of the right of resistance was designed to throw a cloak of legality over the events of 14 July.

Though article one proclaimed that all men were 'equal in rights', it did not assert their political or social equality. It may be doubted, however, whether equality would have been regarded by the authors of the declaration as one of the attributes of human personality and, in any case, the recent abolition of privilege seemed to need no further emphasis. Nor were the liberal aristocrats and moderates in any sense 'levellers'. Nevertheless, clauses VII–IX, dealing with individual liberty, secured the principle of equality before the law, while clauses VI and XIII established, respectively, the principles of civic and fiscal equality.

The doctrine of national sovereignty enunciated in article III abrogated the theory that France was the personal property of its kings and made clear that individuals and corporations alike derived their authority immediately from the nation. The constitutional consequences of this doctrine were stated to be that, since the law was the expression of the general will, all citizens had the right of participating in its formulation either in person, or through their representatives (article VI), that the means of maintaining public order were to be used only for the common advantage (article XII), that the right of consenting to taxation resided in the citizens or their representatives (article XIV), that all public officials were accountable for their administrative acts (article XV) and that the division of powers was indispensable (article XVI). These principles were, therefore, to be the 'fundamentals' of the new constitution.

(v) *The schism in the patriotic party and the October days*

If Louis XVI had acquiesced in the voluntary sacrifices of the liberal aristocracy in August, as he had accepted the popular victory in July, the political horizon would have cleared. Unfortunately, the king refused to surrender the material interests of the clergy and nobility and, by withholding his consent to the August decrees and the Declaration of Rights, gave encouragement once more to the forces of counter-revolution. The reactionary group was also stimulated by political differences, which now arose among the members of the patriotic party. Signs of this cleavage had appeared earlier in the summer, when personal differences had developed between the young and ambitious Barnave and his more mature and moderate colleague, Mounier. After 14 July, when Mounier drew closer to the aristocratic *milieu* of the count de Lally Tollendal and Madame de Tessé, Barnave had formed a working alliance with Alexandre de Lameth and Duport, aristocrats whose liberalism had always been strongly tinged with radicalism. This dissension came to a head when Barnave defended in the Assembly the murders of Berthier and Foullon.[1]

In July and August the conservative group of Mounier drew support from disillusioned members of the liberal aristocracy, whose expectations of leading and controlling the revolution had been upset by the provincial revolts. After 4 August the group had also been joined by clerical deputies, such as Sieyès, who had disapproved of the abolition of ecclesiastical tithes, and by middle-class owners of feudal dues. The political prospects of these moderates, however, depended on their being able to reconcile the monarch and the aristocracy with the revolution. This they hoped to achieve by revising the Declaration of Rights and by making the terms upon which the feudal dues were to be redeemed highly favourable to the aristocracy. Mounier, and those who agreed with him in admiring British constitutional forms, also suggested that the king should be given an absolute veto upon legislation, and that an hereditary second chamber should be established. But the patriotic party, with the exception of Mirabeau, strongly disapproved of the absolute veto, and the smaller provincial nobility, who would have been excluded from the upper chamber, opposed the idea of a bi-cameral legislature. For these reasons the negotiations between the moderates and the Barnave group were broken off on 29 August. This breach

1. Foullon had incurred unpopularity as a member of Breteuil's reactionary ministry and Berthier as *intendant* of Paris. They were murdered in front of the Hôtel de Ville on 23 July.

made possible an agitation in Paris, led by the demagogues Camille Desmoulins and St Huruge, for the transfer of the court and assembly from Versailles to the capital. This dress rehearsal for the events of 5 and 6 October, however, collapsed on 31 August, because it received no support from Barnave and his followers.

Early in September the moderates petitioned the king, in view of the increasing danger from the Parisian mob, to transfer the Assembly to some provincial town, such as Compiègne or Soissons. This advice was rejected. Barnave then persuaded the Assembly, having already converted Necker to the suggestion, to concede the king, not an absolute, but a suspensive veto (11 September). Barnave had understood that, in return, the minister would persuade Louis to withdraw his opposition to the August decrees. Necker, however, afraid that this would encourage the non-payment of taxes, declined to fulfil his share of the bargain. Affairs were now moving to a crisis. When, on 15 September, the Assembly petitioned the king to sanction the decrees, Louis gave orders to the Flanders regiment, stationed at Douai, to march on Versailles.

It was this action which made inevitable the fresh intervention of the Paris mob. The move had been prompted by the clergy, anxious to preserve their tithes, and it had also been made in reliance on the support of the moderate majority in the assembly. Under this renewed threat of counter-revolution, however, the radical wing of the patriotic party let it be known in Paris that this time it would not discountenance a popular rising. The capital was now in the throes of a sharp unemployment crisis caused mainly by the emigration of the nobility since the fall of the Bastille. It was also facing a serious food crisis. It is true that the harvest of 1789 had been a good one, but the fresh supplies, owing to the length of the threshing process, could not reach the markets till late in the winter. Meanwhile, the agrarian revolts had led farmers to hold on to their stocks, hoping for a rise. The efforts of the assembly to counteract local shortages by proclaiming the freedom of the corn trade on 29 August, therefore, had little or no effect. Bread queues in the capital lengthened, the price of food continued to rise and the famine conditions were attributed, not to natural causes, but to the manœuvres of corn speculators and counter-revolutionaries. In these circumstances it was easy for popular agitators to persuade the mob that the food crisis could be solved by invoking the king's assistance against the monopolists. Such intervention would, however, require his presence in the capital.

This economic discontent became politically important because it could now be voiced by a popular newspaper press and ventilated in the sixty electoral assemblies of Paris, which had continued to meet daily since the fall of the Bastille. After the Flanders regiment had been summoned the districts sent deputations to the Commune and pressed the National Assembly for an explanation. Newspapers, such as Marat's *Ami du Peuple*, Loustalot's *Les Révolutions de Paris* and Desmoulins's *La France Libre*, took up the cry for the transference of the court to the capital. Meanwhile, Louis had continued to evade the Assembly's repeated requests for the sanction of the August decrees, playing for time until the arrival of the Flanders regiment. This arrived at Versailles on 29 September, and it was the banquet of official welcome, given in its honour, which touched off the revolt. At this ceremony in the Opera House, the king and queen circulated among the guests, the national cockade was trampled underfoot, and noisy demonstrations made in favour of counter-revolution. As soon as this news reached Paris, popular orators like Camille Desmoulins were easily able to work on the passions of the crowd and to enflame them against the court. On 5 October hundreds of Paris women marched through the rain to Versailles to demand bread, the dismissal of the troops, and the punishment of those who had outraged the tricolour cockade. In turn, the National Guard in Paris forced Lafayette to place himself at its head and follow the crowd to Versailles, where it arrived at night. After the women had invaded the Assembly, Mounier, as president, interviewed the king. Louis, at the last moment, and largely on the advice of Necker, countermanded preparations which had been hastily made for his flight, and, after many hesitations, capitulated to all the popular demands. He took measures for the provisioning of the capital, entrusted himself to the protection of the former French guards, who had been merged in the Paris militia, and sanctioned the August decrees and the Declaration of Rights. The crisis seemed over. The insurgents had obtained satisfaction, Lafayette had taken command of the situation and a return to normal seemed indicated. But on 6 October the revolt flared up again and with more violence. At 6 a.m. the royal *château* was broken into by a furious mob, who had found a workman stretched out with his head split open in the Cour de Marbre. It was this sight which enraged the mob and caused the massacre of the king's bodyguard. The queen narrowly escaped with her life by taking refuge with Louis. The royal guard was saved from annihilation by the appearance of Lafayette with his National

Guards. Once again calm was restored, and when the king and queen appeared with Lafayette on their balcony they were greeted with cheers. Shortly afterwards, however, the crowd took up the cry of 'The King of Paris' and Louis found it impossible to resist. On the same day, the famous and ill-assorted cavalcade made its way to the capital with the royal family as its hostages. Ten days later it was followed by the Assembly.

6

THE WORK OF THE CONSTITUENT ASSEMBLY

AND THE FLIGHT TO VARENNES

(i) *The Constituent Assembly and constructive reform*

The capture of the Bastille had freed the Constituent Assembly from the danger of dissolution; the October days enabled it to resume the task of constructive reform. Various restraints upon its legislative action had now been removed. The moderate party of Mounier, which might have formed itself into an opposition group, seceded from the Assembly in protest against the intervention of the mob. The Orléanist faction had similarly been discredited, and now ceased to exercise a disturbing influence upon the political situation. When the assembly in November found permanent quarters in the *Manège*, or Riding School, near the Tuileries palace, its sittings were no longer subject to the noisy demonstrations of casual spectators, and its legislative freedom ceased to be checked by the imperative mandates. The detailed aspects of constructive legislation were wisely delegated to numerous specialised committees, and better arrangements were made for the conduct of debates. The Declaration of Rights indicated clearly the general objectives of political reform; the municipal revolts had cleared the ground for the improvement of local government; and the fall of privileged corporations made social reconstruction easier. The abundant harvest of 1789, safely garnered, put an end to the food crisis. In these new and favourable conditions, the work of constructive reform could proceed unhampered.

Even before the October rising important decisions of political principle had already been taken. On 9 September the king had been deprived of the right to prorogue or dissolve the future Legislative Assembly and, on 30 September, of the power to initiate legislation.

His effective powers of delay were restricted to the exercise of a suspensive veto, valid for the space of two legislatures.[1] Immediately after the October crisis, Louis' title was altered from 'King of France and of Navarre' to 'King of the French' and henceforth he held office, as the hereditary and inviolable sovereign, by virtue of French constitutional law and not, that is to say, by divine right. With a civil list of 25,000,000 *livres* at his disposal, Louis was already, in theory as well as in effect, a limited constitutional monarch. Freed from the control of the executive and from the supervision of its constituents, the Assembly quickly assumed the omnicompetent authority which had been claimed for it from the outset by Sieyès. Despite the opposition of radicals such as the abbé Grégoire and of Robespierre, the Assembly proceeded to 'usurp national sovereignty for the exclusive benefit of the middle class', by restricting the electoral franchise. In doing so, its action was guided, once more, by the political theory of Sieyès. In July 1789 the abbé had drawn a distinction between 'active' and 'passive' citizenship, the former conferring 'political' rights, such as the exercise of the franchise, and the latter 'civil rights' only. 'Political' rights were regarded by Sieyès, not as inherent rights but rather as functions, the exercise of which would require the fulfilment of certain conditions. These qualifications were defined as adequate education, a modest economic competence and a certain amount of leisure. Similar views had been advocated, it may be noted, before 1789 by the school of Physiocratic thinkers, and they were not inconsistent with the principles set forth in the Declaration of Rights.

Effect was given to these principles by a decree of 22 December 1789, restricting the right to vote, in the primary electoral assemblies and in local municipal elections, to citizens who paid in direct taxes at least the value of three days' labour. For the right to vote in the electoral colleges or to hold municipal office, the prescribed qualification was the payment of ten days' labour in taxes. And finally, eligibility for election as a deputy was made conditional, by a decree of 29 October, on a fiscal payment of a mark's weight in silver (fifty-four francs). The effect of these regulations was that, in a total population of about 26,000,000, just over 4,000,000 Frenchmen could claim the rights of 'active' citizenship, while the final choice of representatives, in the two-stage system of election to the Legislative Assembly, was confined to about 50,000. Thus the political future of France was entrusted to the care of middle-class 'notables'.

1. i.e. four years.

One of the most lasting achievements of the Constituent Assembly was its reform of local government. This was modelled closely upon the scheme of provincial assemblies established by Calonne and Brienne in 1787. Such modifications as were made were rendered necessary by the abolition of the distinction between the separate 'orders' of French society and by the disappearance of the *intendants*. The new local assemblies, created by the laws of 14 and 22 December 1789, were not primarily representative, but administrative bodies, just as the assemblies of 1787 had been. As in 1787, there were three stages of assemblies—the commune replacing the parish and the department taking the place of the province, the intermediate authority being the district. The most striking innovation was that the new authorities, besides dealing with local concerns, were also entrusted with the regional administration of matters of national importance. This increased dose of decentralisation was the result of the municipal revolutions of the previous summer.

France was now divided into eighty-three departments, of approximately equal size, whose boundaries were drawn with great attention to local conditions, and whose names were derived from geographical or natural phenomena. These were subdivided into districts, cantons and communes—the canton being merely an electoral body without real administrative authority. The work of reform was begun from the bottom with the organisation of the communes by the decree of 14 December. It had already been decided to preserve the old village communites, but the need remained to rationalise the diverse and conflicting forms of municipal authority which had resulted from the municipal revolts. Administrative authority was divided between the municipal corporation, consisting of a mayor and a variable number of officials, the general council of the commune and the *procureur* or town clerk. All these authorities were elective and exercised fiscal, police and judicial powers on behalf of the state as well as conducting their own local affairs. In this way, France was covered with a network of about 44,000 autonomous local authorities. The departments and districts were given an administrative framework in the decree of 22 December 1789. In the departments, legislative power was vested in general councils of thirty-six members, elected from those qualified to sit in the electoral colleges. Executive authority was wielded by so-called directories, consisting of eighteen members, elected from the general councils. Analogous institutions with a more restricted membership were established in the districts. The system had its defects—elections occurred too frequently, there was a discrepancy of social structure between the communal and the departmental authorities, the former of which were now elected directly and the latter indirectly, and there was no provision for any form of central control. Such a system could only work effectively, therefore, in times of peace. Sentimentalists have often deplored the uprooting of the traditional and historic provinces, and historians have sometimes maintained that the uniformity of the administrative structure facilitated the transition to the over-central-ised systems of the Jacobins and Napoleon. Modern political theorists urge that the department is too small a unit of administra-tion. Yet the system, in essentials, still remains.

The Assembly began its judicial reforms by abolishing torture on 9 October, and hanging as a form of capital punishment on 1 Decem-ber 1789.[1] On 3 November the *parlements* were, to use the vivid expression of Alexandre de Lameth, 'buried alive', by a decree declaring them to be permanently 'in vacation'.[2] The Assembly then constructed a new form of judicial organisation, which was dovetailed into the new administrative framework by a decree of 16 August 1790. Civil justice was to be dispensed by justices of the peace (*juges de paix*), acting as the agents of the cantonal authority and endeavouring, so far as possible, to settle cases out of court by the use of arbitration. To act as courts of appeal in cases tried by these justices, tribunals consisting of five judges were established in the districts and appeals were allowed to neighbouring district courts. Criminal justice was administered by departmental criminal courts, composed of a president and three judges, and assisted by a trial jury of twelve 'active' citizens chosen by lot. The system was completed by the establishment of a Court of Final Appeal, in both civil and criminal justice (13 May 1790) and of a High Court for treason trials (31 March 1791). Notable features of these reforms were the rejection of the use of the jury in civil cases, the efforts made to combat the excessive litigiousness of suitors, the abolition of the French bar, the popular election of the judges and their payment by the state. It should, perhaps, be noted in passing, that the new criminal procedure did not come into operation until January 1792 and that, in the misguided effort to apply the principle of the division of powers, the prerogative of mercy was withdrawn from the king.

1. Before 1789 capital punishment had taken two forms—decapitation for nobles and hanging for commoners.
2. The *parlement* of Paris was abolished on 15 October 1790.

In financial matters the record of the Constituent Assembly was less impressive. It failed to solve the basic problem of the annual deficit and did not succeed in establishing a modern budgetary system. The suspicion attaching, since the time of Law, to national credit institutions proved too strong for a national bank to be created. Bankruptcy was only avoided by the nationalisation of the ecclesiastical estates and this expedient, unwisely handled, failed to content the peasants and, in time, involved the country in galloping inflation. Against this, however, may be set the reconstruction of the fiscal system which lasted, apart from significant changes made under the executive Directory and the Consulate, until 1914.

The explanation of these failures, in general terms, lies on the surface. The continued existence of the deficit, as Mirabeau so clearly realised, was the Assembly's main security against forcible dissolution. To have established budgetary equilibrium would have been to surrender one of the Assembly's chief political weapons against counter-revolution. Necker himself, however, must bear a large share of the responsibility, for he had throughout grossly underestimated the amount of the deficit, and had given the impression that the destruction of fiscal privilege would suffice to extricate the country from its financial difficulties. Political unrest also militated against the regular collection of revenue, for refusal to pay taxes during the agrarian revolts had gone hand in hand with the refusal of feudal dues. This removed any inducement capitalists may have had to invest in the loans floated by Necker in the autumn of 1789. Nor was it surprising that the minister's efforts to launch a voluntary 'patriotic levy' in September 1789 met with little or no response. By that time the state had hardly sufficient ready money to meet its current expenses and bankruptcy appeared inevitable.

The country had, moreover, to provide for the liquidation of the public debt contracted under the *ancien régime* and the fresh obligations incurred as a result of the Assembly's social and political reforms. The clergy would need to be supported, having been deprived of their tithes, and those whose money had been invested, before 1789, in the purchase of judicial, financial and municipal offices, of which they had since been deprived, would need to be compensated. These were the circumstances which forced the assembly, on 2 November 1789, to decree the nationalisation of the landed estates of the church. This confiscation was justified by the Assembly's agreement to take over the payment of the outstanding clerical debt, to sustain the costs of education, poor relief and public worship formerly defrayed by the church, and to pay clerical salaries. This gigantic operation led to the introduction, on 19 December 1789, of the famous *assignats*. In their original form, these were interest-bearing Treasury bonds, which could be exchanged, on certain conditions, for the church lands now nationalised. After 29 September 1790, however, these instruments ceased to bear interest and became inconvertible paper currency with legal tender status. It was the over-issue of these paper notes in the effort to finance the war with Europe after 1792 which led to their depreciation and to the inflationary crisis of early 1793. For the moment, however, there could be little doubt that their institution had saved the country from immediate bankruptcy.

(ii) *Mirabeau and the monarchy* (*October 1789–April 1791*)

The most formidable contemporary critic of the political and administrative reforms of the Constituent Assembly was Gabriel Honoré de Riqueti, count de Mirabeau, who had been elected member for the Third Estate of Aix in Provence, after being rejected by his own order. The key to an understanding of Mirabeau's activities, between 6 October 1789 and his death on 2 April 1791, is his condemnation of the political radicalism of the Constituent Assembly and his efforts to restore to the executive the power and authority of which it had been deprived. His overriding ambition was to become a minister and his political objective was to endow France with a constitution modelled on that of Great Britain. He was convinced of the profound attachment of his countrymen to monarchical forms and of their hatred of feudal and corporate privileges. The essential work of the revolution he regarded as the destruction of the privileged independence of the church, the *parlements* and the provincial estates, which before 1789 had kept the monarchy in tutelage. His political ideal was a free but limited monarchy, possessed of sufficient strength to restrain the excesses of revolutionary radicalism and to defeat the misguided intrigues of the counter-revolutionaries.

On 23 June 1789, Mirabeau had championed the political independence of the National Assembly, not against the Crown, but against counter-revolution. He had vehemently opposed the assumption of national sovereignty by the third estate on 17 June, and had only taken the Tennis Court Oath under duress. He had been careful to absent himself from the Assembly on the night of 4 August, he had sharply criticised the expediency of drawing up a Declaration of

Rights, and he had vigorously advocated the grant to the king of an
absolute veto over legislation. Mirabeau's campaign for a strong
executive was, therefore, not inconsistent with the political views
which he had openly professed from the outset. The turning-point
of his career was his failure, on 7 November 1789, to prevent the
assembly from excluding deputies from the ministry. It was this
decree which condemned Mirabeau to a career of political intrigue
and prevented his unrivalled political talents and experience from
having their full effect upon the course of events.

The effort to secure the reversal of that decree, to free the king
from his virtual captivity in Paris and to deprive the assembly of the
dictatorial powers which it had assumed henceforth absorbed all
Mirabeau's powers and energy. Utterly lacking in scruple and prepared, if necessary, to risk the evils of civil war in order to achieve
his objectives, Mirabeau found it impossible to secure the confidence
of the queen or the co-operation of the king. Louis disliked his
immorality, Marie Antoinette misunderstood his constant need to
maintain his popularity in the assembly, and neither was completely
satisfied of his sincerity. It is significant that all Mirabeau's own
efforts to effect contact with the court, through the Keeper of the
Seals in July 1789, through the countess d'Ossun, one of the queen's
ladies-in waiting in September, and through the count de Pro ence
after the October days, failed. His secret relations with the court
date from April 1790 and resulted from the initiative of the queen's
political adviser, the count de Mercy-Argenteau, the Austrian ambassador. The nature of the bargain then effected is, in itself, sufficient
explanation of Mirabeau's subsequent failure. The chief intermediary was the count de Lamarck, a Belgian aristocrat, proprietor of a
German regiment in the French service, who had been a hanger-on
at the court and who had known Mirabeau only since 1788. Although
personally devoted to the queen, Lamarck never possessed her entire
trust, as he had been involved in the Belgian revolt against her
brother, the Emperor Joseph II. All Mirabeau's communications
with the court were indirect, and his advice was tendered in the
form of secret notes, transmitted by Lamarck, or by a former almoner
of the queen, the archbishop of Toulouse. Mirabeau only once had a
personal interview with the sovereigns, on 3 July 1790, for this
caused Marie Antoinette so much abhorrence that it was never
repeated. To secure Mirabeau's services, Louis agreed to pay the
orator's outstanding debts amounting to £10,000, to give him a
monthly salary of £300 and to promise him a final honorarium of

£50,000 at the conclusion of the Constituent Assembly, if he fulfilled his engagements. It is clear that the king and queen never respected the man whose conscience they thought they had bought.

Between 1 June 1790 and his death, Mirabeau wrote over fifty secret notes for the court, but his advice was never followed. Nevertheless, by his oratorical triumphs in the Assembly, Mirabeau was able to render valuable services to the monarchy. On 22 May 1790, he preserved for the king the initiative in the right of declaring war, and in February 1791 he prevented further restrictions being placed on Louis' movements after the emigration of the king's aunts to Rome. The ambiguity of Mirabeau's position, however, became more pronounced in December 1790. In that month, he held office as president of the Jacobin club and, at the end of January 1791, he was elected a member of the administration of the department of Paris, and acted, with great personal success, as president of the Constituent Assembly. It was just at this time that, in co-operation with Montmorin, the Foreign Minister, he elaborated his final schemes for the salvation of the monarchy. The essence of the plan, contained in an elaborate memorandum dated 23 December 1790, was to undermine the credit of the National Assembly, to prepare public opinion for a revival of monarchical authority by means of a secret police in Paris and travelling agents in the provinces, and to prepare the way for a revision of the constitution to be effected by a new legislative assembly. The chief defect of this plan was that it could not have remained secret, for its mechanism was too complicated. The court had, moreover, already committed itself to plans for an escape to the eastern frontier without consulting Mirabeau and, indeed, contrary to his repeated warnings. Even if Mirabeau had not died on 2 April 1791, he would not have been able to save the monarchy from the consequences of its own mistakes and miscalculations.

(iii) *The civil constitution of the clergy and religious schism*

The full practical significance of the principle of national sovereignty in the new order was first made clear when the Assembly turned its attention to the relations of church and state. The early reforms affecting the status of religion and the church in France were carried with the agreement and, to some extent, on the initiative of the clergy. On 4 August 1789, the Gallican Church had surrendered its corporate status, its right of self-taxation and the independent administration, which it had defended so tenaciously throughout the eighteenth

century. The influential higher clergy in the Assembly had also
agreed, on 13 February 1790, to the abolition of the contemplative
religious orders. On the whole, the church had accepted the abolition
of ecclesiastical tithes and the alienation of its landed estates, if not
with enthusiasm, at any rate with fortitude and resignation. No
attempt was made to elicit papal condemnation of the sacrifices
imposed by the state, and the Holy See was not consulted about the
reforms sponsored by the French clergy.

Such changes had been largely negative in character. The constructive reforms were contained in a document entitled the 'civil
constitution of the clergy', drafted by the ecclesiastical committee
of the Assembly early in 1790. Its object was not to effect dogmatic
change, but to adapt the forms of the Gallican Church to the newly
created administrative framework and, at the same time, to make
a partial return to the practices of primitive Christianity. The separation of church and state was, at this stage, never contemplated. The
most radical decision was that, henceforth, the ecclesiastical dioceses
were to coincide in extent with the departments. This involved a
reduction in the number of bishoprics from 135 to eighty-three, of
which ten were converted into metropolitan areas. This provision
reflected the Assembly's preoccupation with the idea of administrative
uniformity and represented the converse of the process, by which
the communes had already been assimilated to the parishes. The
second main principle of the civil constitution was that all ecclesiastical offices were to be filled by popular election. Ever since the
Concordat of 1516, the French bishops had been nominated by the
king; in future, they were to be elected, not by the cathedral chapters,
which were now suppressed, but by the 'active' citizens who elected
the other departmental authorities. Similarly, the parish priests were
to be chosen by the electors who nominated the district officials.
Thirdly, the remaining links which had, before 1789, bound the
French bishops to the papacy were now severed, for the newly
elected bishops were to receive spiritual confirmation and canonical
institution from their metropolitans, and were forbidden to recognise
the jurisdictional supremacy of the Holy See. Finally, all French
clerics now became the paid officials of the state, and the opportunity
was taken to increase the salaries of the lower and to decrease those
of the higher clergy. Strict regulations, enforceable by deprivation,
confined the bishops to purely spiritual functions, and imposed on
all clerics the duty of residence in diocese or parish.

The reforms were approved by the Assembly on 12 July 1790,

sanctioned by the king on 22 July, and formally promulgated on 24 August. They were supported by a powerful section of the French episcopate in the Assembly, and it was not anticipated that any serious danger of papal condemnation, or of religious schism, would be involved. The liberal prelates were convinced that Pius VI could be converted to the expediency of making concessions, while the radical reformers considered that his consent could be enforced, if necessary, by threats to annex the papal enclaves in French territory—Avignon and the Venaissin. Nevertheless, it was certain that opposition would be offered by the reactionary bishops, and it soon became clear that the practical difficulties of implementing the reforms would necessitate the adoption of compulsory methods. On 27 November 1790, therefore, the Assembly imposed an all office-holding clergy, on pain of deprivation, an oath requiring them to uphold with all their power the constitution decreed by the National Assembly. This oath was refused by all the bishops except seven and by half the lower clergy, so that by January 1791 the evidence of religious discord could not be ignored. The final schism resulted from the papal condemnation of the civil constitution and the political and social reforms of the revolution in briefs addressed to the French bishops on 10 March and 13 April 1791.

The consequences were far-reaching. The opposition between the 'constitutional' and 'non-juring' or 'refractory' clergy brought into existence rival factions, whose antagonisms were to prove irreconcilable. The schism first made counter-revolution practical politics by providing it with popular support. The severance of relations with the Holy See signalised by the departure of the papal nuncio on 24 May 1791, was not healed till Napoleon's Concordat with the papacy in 1801. It led, in September 1791, to the annexation by the National Assembly of Avignon and the Venaissin, and to the enunciation of the theory of national self-determination. It was Louis XVI's religious scruples, aroused by the papal denunciation, which finally converted him to the necessity of risking his personal safety and the fate of the French monarchy on the chance of a successful escape to the Eastern frontier.

(iv) *The flight to Varennes* (*21 June 1791*)

All the earlier schemes for the king's flight had foundered on Louis' own determination not to desert his post, his memories of the consequences of James II's action, and his suspicion of Orléanist designs on the succession. By the spring of 1791, however, the king's initial hopes that the revolution would exhaust its impetus had evaporated, his sense of guilt at having sanctioned the religious reforms had deepened, and the queen had become convinced of the necessity of provoking foreign intervention. Both the King of Spain and the Emperor had replied to Louis' appeals for assistance that, until the king had publicly condemned the constitution and the royal family was in a place of safety, they could do little. Though there was some force in this argument, it is easy to understand Marie Antoinette's conviction that it was being used as a pretext to justify continued inaction. The flight was, therefore, regarded as one way of forcing the hands of the monarchy's reluctant foreign sympathisers. The queen then suggested that the European sovereigns should call an armed congress near the eastern frontier and should issue a manifesto calling on the Assembly and the nation to revise the constitution and restore Louis to his rightful position. It was assumed that, after Louis' escape, he could then assume the role of mediator between the nation and the hostile powers and might thus hope to be welcomed back on his own terms by a grateful, or intimidated Assembly. These plans, however, evoked little enthusiasm at Vienna, for both the Emperor Joseph II and his successor, Leopold, frankly advised Louis to make his own peace with the revolutionaries and accept the reforms, which were so closely similar to those they had sponsored in their own dominions. The queen's suspicions thus seemed to have been confirmed. The final decision to escape to Montmédy on the eastern frontier seems to have been taken after the king had been prevented by a popular revolt from receiving the sacraments at St Cloud from a non-juring priest during Holy Week.

The arrangements for the flight were made by the queen's admirer, the Swedish count Axel de Fersen and the marquis de Bouillé, whose military command extended over the north-eastern frontier areas, and whose headquarters were at Metz. Bouillé's original plan was that the king should travel separately in a fast coach, that no military escorts should be provided *en route*, and that the escape should be in charge of a resourceful and determined officer capable of dealing with unforeseen accidents. The queen, however, insisted that the whole royal family should travel together, and, to allay the anxieties of the Emperor Leopold, it was decided that Bouillé should provide military detachments to protect the fugitives once they had entered the area of his command. These alterations were partly responsible for the failure of the project. The presence of the king's sister, Madame Elisabeth, the queen and her two children necessitated the inclusion in the royal party of two sewing women and the children's governess, Madame de Tourzel. Though the domestics travelled in a cabriolet, the rest could only be accommodated in a commodious travelling coach, whose speed, when fully loaded, was not more than seven miles an hour. It was finally decided that the party should travel by way of Châlons, Pont de Somme Vesle, Sainte-Menehould, Clermont, Varennes, Dun and Stenay. The Emperor agreed to concentrate Austrian troops at Arlon near Luxembourg, and the presence of these forces was to be used by Bouillé as the pretext for the formation of a camp at the king's destination, Montmédy. The military detachments along the route were to be explained to the local inhabitants as escorts for the passage of a 'treasure' on its way to the troops posted on the frontier. Relays of horses for the coaches were available at all the regular stages, except at Varennes, and there special arrangements were made for fresh horses to await the king on the outskirts of the village.

The escape from Paris was planned by Fersen. He borrowed large sums on the king's behalf and transmitted them to Bouillé, he purchased and specially fitted out the travelling coach belonging to a Russian friend, the baroness de Korff. Madame de Tourzel was to impersonate the baroness and travel under a forged passport signed by Louis, while the king and queen were to assume the parts of valet and governess. Fersen had regular access to the queen's apartments in the Tuileries through a door, which Lafayette knew to be unguarded, and it was through this that the escape was made late on the night of 20 June. Fersen himself helped to drive the royal coach out of Paris as far as Bondy.

The journey was a chapter of accidents and miscalculations. Once Paris had been left behind the fugitives considered themselves safe and little effort was made to maintain the pre-arranged time schedule or to evade recognition. The result was that the coach did not reach Pont de Somme Vesle, the first stage where an escort was stationed, till six in the evening. Here the duke de Choiseul had been waiting with his detachment of hussars since two in the afternoon. His troops had aroused suspicion and the duke had withdrawn them at four o'clock and had sent back a message to the other military commanders that the royal coach was not to be expected that day. In this way, the arrangements made for the escorts collapsed. Meanwhile, the king had been recognised at Châlons and when the coach reached Sainte-Menehould, he was again recognised by the posting-master Drouet. Though the latter allowed the party to proceed

without asking for passports, the civic authorities soon discovered
the identity of the travellers, owing to the incautious behaviour of the
commander of the escorts. Drouet was immediately despatched on
horseback to overtake the fugitives. When the coach arrived at
Varennes it was pitch dark, the relays of horses had been moved, and
half an hour was lost in searching for them. This gave Drouet and
his companion time to overtake the coach, to arouse the inhabitants and to block the bridge over the Aire at the end of the village.
Once the royal party had been forced to dismount from the coach and
the king had been identified, his irresolution prevented any further
attempt to escape.

The immediate reaction to the news of the king's escape from Paris
was a general expectation of civil war and foreign intervention. In
the provinces, there was a recrudescence of the same 'Great Fear'
which had swept over the country in the summer of 1789. The king's
capture at Varennes did little to reassure public opinion, for his
brother, the count de Provence, had made good his escape to Belgium and there had been a wholesale emigration of the officers of
the frontier regiments. Gustavus III of Sweden recalled all his
subjects from France, Charles IV of Spain expelled Frenchmen by
the thousand, and Catherine II of Russia insulted the French
ambassador.

The Assembly, however, faced the crisis calmly. It immediately
took over the executive government and resolved that its decrees
should be valid without the royal sanction. On 21 June it declared
itself in permanent session, closed the frontiers, and later despatched
three commissioners—Barnave, Pétion and Latour-Maubourg—to
meet the king on his return journey and accompany him back to the
capital. On 24 June the elections for the new Legislative Assembly
were suspended, the fortresses placed in a state of defence and the
army put on a war footing. On 27 June an appeal was made for
100,000 volunteers. Meanwhile, on 25 June, when the royal family
arrived back in Paris, the Assembly suspended Louis from his functions. By not acceding to the demands of the radical political clubs
for the king's immediate deposition, or for the establishment of a
provisional executive council, the Assembly clearly indicated that
it intended to restore Louis as soon as it was safe to do so. To have
deposed the king at that stage would have exposed the country to the
dangers of foreign intervention. This danger was emphasised on 6
July when the Emperor issued from Padua a circular note to the
European powers, in which he urged concerted action 'to vindicate

the liberty and honour of the most Christian King and his family and to limit the dangerous extremes of the French revolution'. It seemed as if the failure of the king's flight had at last roused the Emperor to a sense of his responsibilities.

(v) *The 'massacre' of the Champ de Mars (17 July 1791)*

It was only natural that the Assembly should have been more influenced by this growing external danger than by the radical petitions of the Cordelier club and fraternal societies. These had now raised the demand that the king's fate should be submitted to a popular referendum. On 15 July, however, Barnave induced the Assembly to exonerate the sovereigns and to institute proceedings against Bouillé and his accomplices, who were alleged to have 'kidnapped' the royal family. These decisions of the National Assembly were accepted by the Jacobin club but not by the Cordelier club and the fraternal societies, who organised a demonstration in favour of the king's dethronement. On 15 July, under this popular pressure, a section of the Jacobin club had agreed to promote such a petition to the Assembly. The drafting of this petition was left to Brissot and Choderlos de Laclos, who inserted a clause alluding to the necessity of a Regency. This was regarded by the republicans as a manœuvre in favour of the duke of Orléans and, on 17 July, a fresh petition was drafted by the officials of the Cordelier club on the Champ de Mars. While this republican petition was being signed on the altar, which had been erected a few days before for the celebration of the fall of the Bastille, two men were discovered under the steps leading up to the platform. It was immediately assumed that these luckless individuals were counter-revolutionaries and they were put to death by the infuriated crowd. This incident and an assault on an *aide-de-camp* of Lafayette brought on the scene Bailly, the mayor of Paris, Lafayette and the National Guard, preceded by a red flag—the sign that the municipality had decided to enforce martial law. It was evening by this time and the crowd assembled in the Champ de Mars numbered over 6,000. A shot was fired from the mob, and Lafayette ordered his guards to retaliate. Several volleys were fired into the crowd, about fifty of the petitioners were killed and order thus restored.

This volley, however, put an end to the political influence and popularity of Lafayette and also wrecked the subsequent career of Bailly. The 'massacre' provided the republican cause with its first martyrs and did much to discredit the victory of the moderates. Its

most significant result, however, was a schism in the Jacobin club.
Those members who had disapproved of the petition for the king's
dethronement seceded from the society and founded a rival organisation known as the Feuillant club, to which only 'active' citizens
were admitted. But for the strenuous efforts made by Robespierre
in its defence, it seems unlikely that the Jacobin club would have
survived this crisis.

(vi) *The Feuillants and constitutional revision*

The days of the Constituent Assembly were now numbered. It still remained, however, to incorporate decrees into the formal instrument
of the constitution. This gave the new Moderate or 'Feuillant' party,
led by Barnave, Duport and Alexandre de Lameth, the chance
denied to Mirabeau of revising the constitution in a sense more
favourable to the monarchy. The means employed, however, were
still the same—intrigue with the court. Barnave, who had forfeited
much of his influence with the radicals by his defence of the interests
of the colonial planters, now made a belated return to the political
faith of his former associate, Mounier. He conceived it to be his
mission to end the revolution before the middle classes were confronted by an attack on property, to reconcile the monarchy with the
nation before the *émigrés* could ruin the chances of its survival, and
to pacify the European sovereigns before their coalition could challenge the nascent force of French nationalism. During the return
journey from Varennes he had managed to acquaint the queen with
his conversion, and early in July he began a secret correspondence
with her in the effort to implement his plans. His advice was that the
king should loyally accept the constitution after it had been revised,
and that the queen should induce the Emperor Leopold to desert
the cause of the *émigrés*. In this way, Louis could help to stem the
progress of the republican movement and Leopold might hope to
prevent the liberal principles of the revolution spreading to his
dominions. If the *émigrés* could be persuaded to return and the Emperor to revive the Franco-Austrian alliance, the credit for the
pacification would redound to the monarchy.

The campaign of the Feuillants in the Assembly for the revision of
the constitution in a conservative sense achieved only limited success.
The right of electing deputies in the electoral colleges was now confined to owners or occupiers of property valued on the taxation
rolls at between 150 and 400 days' labour, according to the locality.
This further restriction of the electorate, however, was offset by

making all 'active' citizens eligible for election as deputies—a concession to Robespierre, who had from the outset virulently criticised the 'silver mark' qualification. In fact, however, these alterations in the electoral system were never applied, since the elections for the Legislative Assembly were resumed in August and were held under the original arrangements. A more significant change was the provision that the civil constitution of the clergy should be removed from the constitution. This meant that the Legislative Assembly would be able to revise or amend the religious settlement, though it could not amend the constitution. It also meant that the oath of fidelity to the constitution exacted of beneficed clergy would no longer pose any question of religious scruple. The way thus seemed open for a healing of the religious schism. The Feuillants, nevertheless, failed to obtain the consent of the assembly for the establishment of a second chamber; they failed to rescind the decree excluding deputies from the ministry; and they failed to abrogate the decree of 16 May 1791, excluding members of the Constituent Assembly from the new Legislative Assembly.

A more serious obstacle to the success of Barnave's broader policy was, however, his inability to secure the confidence of the king and queen. Marie Antoinette continued to intrigue with the Emperor and made little effort to bring pressure on the *émigrés*. It was partly at her instigation that, on 27 August 1791, a declaration was signed at Pillnitz by the Emperor and the King of Prussia. In this proclamation, the sovereigns jointly declared that, having heard the views of the *émigré* princes, they regarded the situation of the King of France as 'an object of interest to all the sovereigns of Europe'. They also expressed the hope that the powers would unite to establish in France a monarchical system which would be equally reconcilable with the rightful authority of the sovereigns and with the welfare of the French nation. If the powers consented to do this, the contracting parties announced that they would then take active and prompt measures to secure the end proposed, and that, in the meantime, they would keep their forces in readiness. Those who were aware of Great Britain's firm adherence to neutrality at this point could appreciate that the conditional clause in the declaration merely underlined the Emperor's reluctance to intervene at the instigation of the *émigrés*. In France, however, it was generally assumed that Great Britain would be glad of an excuse to revenge herself for French interference in the American war, and the declaration was regarded as gratuitously provocative. A simultaneous manifesto of the *émigré* princes urging Louis to refuse his consent to the new constitution and threatening the revolutionaries with condign punishment if they harmed the king, confirmed the impression that a hostile concert of European powers was about to be formed. Louis had the good sense not to follow this advice, for on 14 September 1791 he publicly accepted the constitution which had been finally approved by the Assembly on 3 September. The labours of the Constituent Assembly were now over and it broke up at the end of the month.

7

THE LEGISLATIVE ASSEMBLY, WAR AND
THE LAST DAYS OF THE MONARCHY

(i) *The political consequences of the Constitution of 1791*

The criticisms of the Constitution of 1791 made by Mirabeau and Barnave were amply justified during the lifetime of the Legislative Assembly, which sat from 1 October 1791 to 20 September 1792. The new Assembly, elected on a restricted middle-class franchise, was deprived of the broad basis of political authority upon which its predecessor had securely rested. The exclusion of former members of the Constituent Assembly not only robbed it of much painfully acquired political experience, but also led to the growth of rival political authorities. Pétion, who replaced Bailly as mayor of Paris in November, Danton, as assistant deputy of the town clerk, and Robespierre, as public prosecutor of the department of Paris, did much to extend the power and influence of the municipality and to develop the activity of the political clubs. It is significant that the most vital issue of foreign policy at this time—war or peace with Europe —was fought out as much in the Jacobin club as in the Legislative Assembly, and that the most important issue of domestic politics— the fate of the monarchy—was decided by the Parisian sections. Similarly, the continued exclusion from ministerial office of members of the legislature meant that the period was one of excessive ministerial instability. With few exceptions, the ministers were political cyphers. If freely chosen by the king, they tended to be counter-revolutionaries, and so arouse the distrust of the Assembly; if forced on the king by the Assembly, they were circumvented by the court. The issue of the royal veto now became a central political issue, and the knowledge that the veto was often applied on the advice of secret counsellors, such as Barnave, discredited the main constitutional means of preserving the royal authority. The Constitution of 1791 would have been workable only if the king's acceptance of it had been genuine: the lip-service paid to it by Louis deceived no one, and the truth was that the limited constitutional monarchy envisaged by the Constituent Assembly was never given a proper trial.

(ii) Political groupings in the Legislative Assembly

The strongest political group in the Legislative Assembly, at least numerically, consisted of members of the Feuillant club. In December 1791 no less than 264 of the 745 members of the Assembly belonged to this newly formed rival of the Jacobin club. The political views of this section were those advocated by the so-called Triumvirate of Barnave, Alexandre de Lameth and Duport.[1] Barnave continued to urge that the king should take every opportunity of exhibiting his loyalty to the Constitution. He pleaded for the formation of a harmonious and active ministry for the maintenance of peace at all costs. With this end in view, he not only did his best to dissuade the Emperor from further intervention in French affairs, but also offered the émigrés every inducement to return. At this time, the Feuillants exercised greater control over the Parisian newspaper press than the Jacobins—their main organs being the Chronique de Paris and the Gazette Universelle. Among their paid journalists was the poet André Chénier. Their supporters inside the Parisian electoral assembly were more numerous than those of the left-wing political groups, and were more strongly organised in the club de Sainte-Chapelle. Opportunity was taken at the end of October 1791, on the resignation of Montmorin, to reconstruct the ministry and the newcomers were, in the main, sympathetic to the policy of the Feuillants. De Lessart, who replaced Montmorin at the Foreign Office, was a protégé of Necker, and had already been Controller-General and Minister of the Interior. Despite this, he was a figure of no political consequence, and soon encountered the open hostility of the radical groups in the Assembly. The only minister to possess the king's confidence was Bertrand de Molleville, Minister of Marine, a former intendant and a conservative partisan of the Austrian alliance. The Minister of the Interior, Cahier de Gerville, the Minister of Finance, Tarbé, and the Minister of Justice, Duport du Tertre, were all makeshifts. The dominating influence in the ad-

1. Charles Lameth was almost as influential a member of this group as his brother, so that the label 'Triumvirate' was a misnomer.

ministration, after his appointment as Minister of War early in December, was count Louis de Narbonne. An illegitimate son of Louis XV, Narbonne had been brought up at Court, but had early espoused the cause of the revolution. He had escorted the King's aunts on their hazardous journey to Rome in February 1791, and in the following September he had been appointed, thanks to his friendship with Lafayette, to the command of the professional *corps d'élite* of the National Guard of Paris with the rank of brigadier. It was Madame de Staël, whose lover he was, who had encouraged his political ambitions, and who had induced both Barnave and Montmorin to recommend his appointment as minister.

The power of the Feuillants, nevertheless, rested on insecure foundations. Their leaders, Barnave, Alexandre de Lameth, Duport, Bailly and Lafayette, were all excluded from the Assembly as ex-constituents, and the last two were uneasy allies of the Triumvirate. Lafayette still professed a somewhat juvenile republicanism, and suspected that Barnave and his associates were too disposed to make concessions to the aristocracy. Barnave's secret relations with the queen also distracted his attention from the problems of political leadership and, once they had become known, gave rise to rumours that the Feuillants were in league with the counter-revolutionaries. The queen only tolerated Barnave as a temporary champion and consistently disregarded his advice. The Feuillant club itself proved a mushroom growth, and did not long survive the regulation made by the Assembly in December 1791 that no political club should be allowed to hold meetings within its precincts. In so far as the Feuillants still believed in the possibility of establishing a second chamber, and of abolishing the Civil Constitution of the clergy, they were cherishing an impractical political faith. In so far as they were working for a pacific solution of international difficulties by a closer understanding with Austria, they were liable to general misrepresentation and distrust at a time when anti-Austrian feeling in the Assembly was rising rapidly.

Less numerous, but far more active, were the left-wing deputies, 136 of whom joined the Jacobin club after October. Like the Feuillants, the Jacobins had their supporters in the electoral assembly of the capital, meeting as a club at the Bishop's palace under the presidency of Dubois-Crancé. Like the Feuillants also, the left-wing politicians represented two distinct political tendencies. The extreme radicals, who formed the nucleus of the future republican party, were more powerful in the Jacobin and Cordelier clubs than in the

Assembly. Their leaders were men like Merlin de Thionville, Chabot, Couthon and Cambon. The dominating group of the left-wing deputies of the Legislative Assembly consisted of the followers of Jacques Pierre Brissot. During the Legislative Assembly these men were known as *Brissotins* and during the Convention as *Girondins*, owing to the fact that several of their best-known representatives, such as Vergniaud, Grangeneuve and Ducos, came from the department of the Gironde. As compared with the members of the Constituent Assembly, the Brissotins were, on the whole, younger and of less assured social status. Nevertheless, they were mostly journalists, lawyers and merchants, and their main political contacts were with the world of commerce and finance and with foreign refugees from Switzerland, Belgium and Holland. One may, at this period, think of the Brissotins as a new type of French professional politician with an eye on political advancement and an interest concentrated on foreign rather than on domestic affairs. If the Feuillants were the party of peace, the Brissotins soon distinguished themselves from the rest of the Jacobins by their passionate advocacy of war. It was this forward policy, the oratorical gifts of Vergniaud, Gensonné and Guadet, and the skilled political leadership of Brissot, which enabled this group to dominate the 350 members of the centre of the Assembly who, on domestic issues, stood nearer to the ground occupied by the Feuillants.

(iii) *The origins of the war of 1792*

The possibility of war with Europe had existed ever since the king's escape to Varennes, if only for the reason that the stricter confinement of the sovereigns in the capital confirmed Marie Antoinette in her views that the sole hope of salvation for the monarchy lay in foreign intervention. The king's acceptance of the constitution in September was a formal act, the effective results of which remained to be seen. For the moment, it merely stimulated further the reactionary fervour of the *émigrés*. By her continued intrigues the queen early aroused the suspicions of the Legislative Assembly and provoked a wave of anti-Austrian feeling, which did much to impair good relations with the Emperor and to undermine the influence of the Feuillants.

In contrast with the Feuillants' efforts to reconcile the refractory priests and to conciliate the Emperor, the Brissotins set out to repress the ecclesiastical counter-revolution and to intimidate the *émigrés*. Their first move in this direction was the passing of a decree on 31

October, summoning the count de Provence to return to France within three months, upon pain of forfeiting his rights to the succession. This, however, only produced a belated and evasive reply from the prince in December. The next step was taken on 9 November, when the Assembly decreed that all *émigrés* who had not repatriated themselves by 1 January 1792, would be treated as traitors. Their goods would thus be subject to confiscation and, if caught, their lives would be forfeit. Though the *émigré* Court at Coblentz, now guided by Calonne, had undoubtedly been partly responsible for the Declaration of Pilnitz, and though the military forces of counter-revolution under the Prince de Condé at Worms were assuming greater coherence, it can hardly be considered that the threat represented by the *émigrés* was in itself a serious one. On the other hand, the effect of the emigration on the financial and commercial situation in France and on the discipline in the army could not be ignored. More disturbing were the administrative and political results of the religious schism. The difficulties attending the establishment of the constitutional church continued, and the local administrative authorities were now bringing pressure to bear on the Assembly to maintain stricter control over the activities of the refractory priests. Acting on the instructions of the emigrant bishops, the non-juring clergy were discouraging the faithful not only from purchasing the confiscated estates of the church, but also from paying their taxes. Most of the members of the Legislative Assembly had been drawn from the ranks of the new administrative hierarchy and were, therefore, particularly susceptible to this pressure from the local authorities. Then, too, only twenty-six members of the Legislative Assembly were clergy and all of them belonged to the new constitutional church. These circumstances explain the passing, on 29 November, of a decree, the form of which reflected the peculiar complexity of the religious issues of the moment. In its essential provisions the decree may be said to have offered a *modus vivendi*, but its sanctions were so severe as to amount to persecution. The decree exacted from the non-juring clergy a new civil oath of loyalty to the nation, the law and the king. As the new oath was purely political, it allowed the non-juring clergy to acquire legal status without violating their consciences. On the other hand, all priests who refused to take the new oath were declared 'suspect' of treasonable intentions, were deprived of their ecclesiastical pensions and were made subject to ejection from their homes and to imprisonment by the departmental authorities.

Though the decrees of 9 and 29 November were vetoed by the
king in December on the advice of the Feuillant leaders, the Brissotins continued with their policy of legislating against the agents of
counter-revolution. Under pressure from this quarter and on the
advice of Narbonne, the king announced in the Assembly on 14
December that he would summon the elector of Trêves to disband the
armed gatherings of *émigrés* at Coblentz before 15 January 1792, and
that he would declare war on the elector if he refused to give satisfaction. To show that this was not an empty threat, Narbonne
announced that three French armies would be formed under the
command of Rochambeau, Lückner and Lafayette. The elector of
Trêves, glad of the excuse of ridding himself of his unwelcome guests,
and conscious of the Emperor's lukewarm support of the *émigrés*,
replied without delay that he was willing to carry out Louis' wishes.

That these events did not bring about a relaxation of the tension
between France and Austria may be attributed, on the one hand, to
a sudden stiffening of the Emperor Leopold's attitude and, on the
other, to the military and political schemes of Narbonne. Even before
the French pressure on the elector of Trêves, Leopold had revived the
question of the feudal rights of the imperial princes in Alsace. In
accordance with the decrees of 4–11 August 1789, the feudal dues of
the German princes with possessions in Alsace had either been
abolished or made subject to redemption. In reply to this unilateral
action taken by the Constituent Assembly, the German princes had
refused to discuss the matter of compensation and had appealed to
the Imperial Diet. After long hesitations, the Frankfort Diet had
finally issued, on 21 July 1791, a decree or *conclusum*, upholding the
claims of the princes. On 3 December the Emperor informed Louis
XVI in a despatch that he intended to ratify the decision of the
Imperial Diet, which he did a week later. This issue, which had
seemed likely to become extinct, was thus revived. More provocative
was an imperial dispatch, dated 21 December 1791, in which the
Emperor, while approving the dispersal of the *émigrés* at Coblentz,
announced that he had ordered Marshal Bender, commander-in-
chief of the Imperial troops in the Netherlands, to protect the elector
of Trêves, if the need arose, from any incursions on his territory by
undisciplined French forces. This action was supported by the argument that the French government was no longer master of the
situation on its own soil.

That there was some substance in these contentions is shown by
the fact that, on 21 December, Narbonne had set out on a tour of

the north-eastern frontier districts in order to tighten up the discipline of the troops. In three weeks, Narbonne practically put a stop to emigration in the army, raised its morale and returned to the Assembly with plans for raising 50,000 new recruits by fusing the National Guards with the regiments of the line. These plans, however, proved premature and Narbonne soon concluded that the army could only be cured of the evils with which the revolution had afflicted it if it were tested in a limited war with the Rhineland electors. The protection offered by the Emperor to the elector of Trêves, however, threatened to transform the punitive expedition which Narbonne had in mind into a more general conflict. This situation forced Narbonne into an alliance of convenience with the Brissotins, with whom he had come to agree in thinking that France's real enemy was not the *émigrés* but Austria. It also induced him, at the suggestion of Madame de Staël, to set on foot negotiations with the idea of ensuring Prussian neutrality and an alliance with Great Britain. At the end of December 1791 the count de Ségur was dispatched on an official mission to Berlin with instructions to dissuade the King of Prussia from supporting the Emperor. Meanwhile, the son of Marshal Custine was commissioned to pay a secret visit to Frederick II's great captain, the duke of Brunswick, in order to offer him the post of generalissimo of the French armies. In January 1792 Talleyrand, a personal friend of Narbonne's, was sent on an unofficial mission to London to prepare the ground for a Franco-British understanding. All these overtures were rebuffed. Ségur's mission was wrecked by the agents of the *émigrés* and by Louis XVI's secret repudiation of his envoy, Custine's by the caution of the duke of Brunswick, and Talleyrand's by his intrigues with the parliamentary opposition and by the British Government's mistrust of his proposals.

The secret political design upon which these diplomatic manœuvres hinged was that the constitutional revision envisaged by the Feuillants should be effected by means of an army victorious in war, which could then be employed in the interest of the monarchy. Narbonne was thus the first to contemplate ending the revolution and restoring order by a military dictatorship. These plans, however, involved the minister in a situation which soon got out of control. His scheme for a limited war against the elector of Trêves alienated Barnave, who early in 1792 finally realised the hopelessness of his attempts to guide the queen and retired from the political scene. Narbonne's alliance with the Brissotins also had the effect of stimulating the rising demand in the country, not for a military promenade in the Rhineland, but for a full-scale war with Austria. Ever since October 1791 Brissot had been preaching an ideological war of peoples against sovereigns, and the war with Austria was envisaged as one in which France would be assisted by the subject races of the Habsburg dominions. In this illusion the Brissotins were encouraged by refugee patriots from Belgium, Liège, Holland and Switzerland. In January 1792 Robespierre, at the Jacobin club, did his best to expose the preparations for a military dictatorship made by Narbonne and to dissuade the war-mongers from becoming 'armed missionaries', but he only succeeded in widening the breach between the Brissotins and his own followers. It is perhaps worth noting, in passing, that Robespierre, at this point, was neither an unqualified pacifist, nor a covert collaborationist. He was merely contending that counter-revolution should be defeated in France before its protectors abroad were assailed. Marat, too, argued in the same sense, but his influence was diminished by the fact that his popular newspaper, *L'Ami du Peuple*, had temporarily ceased to appear in the middle of December 1791.

A fresh stage in the events leading to war opened in the middle of January 1792 when Gensonné, in the name of the diplomatic committee of the Assembly, raised the question whether the Emperor's orders to Marshal Bender could be reconciled with the Franco-Austrian treaty of 1756. On 25 January, the Assembly decided to challenge the Emperor on this point. It invited Louis to ask Leopold whether he still regarded himself as an ally of the French nation and whether he renounced all engagements directed against French sovereign independence and the stability of the French constitution. If no answer were received to this inquiry before 1 March, France would feel compelled to declare war on Austria. From this point, all de Lessart's efforts, as Foreign Minister, to tone down the asperity of the notes which subsequently passed between Paris and Vienna only played into the hands of the Brissotins, who now determined to overthrow the Feuillant government by exposing the almost criminal weakness of its diplomacy. Meanwhile, on 7 February, the Emperor had succeeded in procuring the King of Prussia's signature to a treaty of defensive alliance, the preliminaries of which had been concluded in the previous July. In this treaty the two powers agreed to afford each other mutual aid and assistance and to promote a concert of other powers for the settlement of French affairs. Though the question of a possible further partition of Poland continued to divide the allies, and though the treaty did not protect the most vulnerable parts of Austrian and Prussian territory, it persuaded the Austrian chancellor, Kaunitz, that France could safely be hectored into submission. Hence it was that Franco-Austrian diplomacy in February and March of 1792 consisted merely of an exchange of mutual recrimination and abuse.

The final phase of these rapidly deteriorating relations opened on 10 March, when Louis XVI abruptly dismissed Narbonne and news was received in Paris of the death of the Emperor Leopold. Narbonne had virtually brought about his own fall by intriguing against the king's favourite minister, de Molleville, and by threatening Louis with the combined resignations of Rochambeau, Lückner and Lafayette. The king's action, however, provided the Brissotins with the excuse for impeaching de Lessart, and for denouncing the other members of the Feuillant administration. In this way, the ministry was overthrown and the Brissotins were left to construct one of their own. The Department of Foreign Affairs was given to Dumouriez, that of Finance to Clavière, a Swiss banker and former collaborator of Mirabeau, the Ministry of the Interior to Roland de la Platière, a civil servant, the Navy and Colonies to Lacoste, and the Ministry of Justice to Duranthon. Narbonne's place was taken by de Grave—a nonentity. The chief figure in the new government was Dumouriez, a fanatical opponent of Austria, ambitious and determined on war. The change of Austrian rulers also brought war nearer, for the successor of the cautious and pacific Leopold was Francis II, young, impetuous and with a taste for military adventure. His very youth threw him into the hands of the Imperial Chancellor Kaunitz, who was determined to humiliate France by threatening her with the newly concluded alliance with Prussia. It soon became clear, moreover, that Francis had made up his mind to champion the cause of the Alsatian princes and the Pope, and to secure some guarantee of strong government in France.

In some respects, the policy of Dumouriez proved to be identical with that of his predecessor. He had the same conviction that Austria could be isolated by means of understandings with Prussia and Great Britain, and hoped that he might even be able to induce the German princes not to elect Francis as emperor. Like Narbonne, he secretly regarded war as an effective means of restoring the monarchical authority of Louis XVI. As a former agent of Louis XV's secret diplomacy, however, Dumouriez inherited from the *ancien régime* a bitter hatred of the Austrian alliance, and was convinced that the German powers intended to treat France as a second Poland. As soon as he became Foreign Minister, Dumouriez adopted a challenging and uncompromising attitude towards Vienna and pushed on with active preparations of war. Whereas, however, Narbonne had contemplated a French offensive on the Moselle and the Rhine, directed on Trêves and Mayence, Dumouriez laid plans for overrunning the Low Countries. His object there was not formal annexation, for that would have antagonised Great Britain, but the establishment of a Belgian federal republic. The attack was to be justified to the British ministers on the ground of military necessity, and it was intended that the French armies should live on the country and thus relieve the pressure on French finances. One of Dumouriez's first acts was to dispatch Maret—the future duke of Bassano—as an agent to incite the Belgians to revolt. Custine was once again charged with the duty of separating Prussia from Austria, and Talleyrand was entrusted with the task of preparing the way for a prospective alliance with England. The suggestions which were put to the British Government were bold and imaginative. As the basis of the alliance, Dumouriez offered to draw up a new commercial treaty, to surrender Tobago and co-operate in the liberation of the Spanish American colonies. Great Britain, France and possibly the United States were together to share the opportunities for great commercial ventures, which would thus be opened up. The aggresive continental ambitions of Austria, Prussia and Russia could be checked, and the peace of Europe guaranteed by means of a balance between the liberal powers of the West and the autocratic monarchies of the East. It was the same policy which Talleyrand was to champion with success after a quarter of a century of conflict at the Congress of Vienna in 1815.

These grandiose plans and calculations, however, soon came to grief. Custine's mission in Berlin was futile from the start, since the King of Prussia was obsessed with the danger from revolutionary France. Throughout Europe, Dumouriez's diplomacy was frustrated by the secret agents employed by the baron de Breteuil, who was now working in close association with Fersen and the Count de Mercy-Argenteau. The Austro-Prussian combination proved unbreakable, while the duke of Brunswick showed his real sympathies by accepting the post of commander-in-chief of the combined anti-French forces. As the interchange of notes between Paris and Vienna degenerated in the course of March into a series of ultimata, war became inevitable. On 20 April 1792, war on the 'King of Hungary and Bohemia' was declared on the proposition of Louis XVI in the Legislative

Assembly, before Talleyrand had set out for London. Only seven votes were cast against the motion.

(iv) *The last days of the monarchy*

In pressing for war with Austria, the Brissotins had calculated that the Belgians would revolt, that Hohenzollern jealousy of the house of Habsburg would render the Austro-Prussian alliance ineffective and that the conflict would prove for France a short and victorious one. If this expectation was almost immediately falsified, the Brissotins' hopes that the war would expose the treasonable activities of the French Court were, however, abundantly fulfilled. Louis XVI and Marie Antoinette had welcomed the outbreak of war in the expectation that it would lead to French reverses and to the invasion of the country by the combined armies of Austria and Prussia. As the Brissotins had foreseen, the open complicity of the king and queen with the enemy in time of war could have only one result, if national defeat was to be avoided, and that was the downfall of the monarchy.

On the outbreak of hostilities the French armies were totally unprepared for active military operations. The gaps in the ranks of their officers caused by emigration had not been filled, only about one-third of the 100,000 volunteers from the National Guard had responded to the appeal made after the flight to Varennes, and the troops in the field numbered only 130,000 in all. The discipline of these troops had been undermined by a series of military revolts in the course of 1790, and their equipment was defective. No preparations had been made for gearing the economy of the country to war conditions, and the spring of 1792 had brought a serious depreciation of the assignats. As soon as the French armies began active operations, they sustained a series of defeats. Under Dumouriez's instructions, three armies had been formed, one under Custine in Alsace to guard the Swiss frontier, one under Lafayette at Metz, and the third under Rochambeau at Valenciennes. Part of the latter, under the command of Biron, had orders to move on Brussels, the operation to be assisted by detachments from Lafayette's forces. An army corps under General Dillon at Lille was directed to attack Tournai. No sooner had Dillon's troops advanced beyond the border than they were surprised by Austrian detachments. A partial withdrawal ended in confusion and the French forces were quickly involved in a precipitate retreat on Lille, in the course of which the cry of 'treason' was raised and Dillon massacred by his own troops. Biron got no farther than Mons before coming upon the Austrians and although outnumbering the enemy he, too, ordered a retreat. Two days later, he was back in Valenciennes with his forces completely demoralised. In these circumstances Lafayette refused to advance, Rochambeau offered his resignation, and his criticisms of Dumouriez's strategy was supported by the other generals.

These disasters reacted immediately upon the political situation in France. Their first effect was to restore the personal prestige and authority of Robespierre, whose previous criticisms of the war policy of the Brissotins had undermined his popularity. Robespierre pressed home the advantage by founding his own newspaper— *The Defender of the Constitution*—in which he attacked the generals in the field and the Brissotins in the Assembly. This re-emergence of Robespierre as a popular leader was a factor of the highest importance in the political situation which led to the downfall of the monarchy. The second result of the military reverses was to redouble popular suspicion of the court and particularly of the queen. Paris was soon full of stories of an alleged 'Austrian Committee' operating from the Tuileries. On 15 May Isnard, a prominent Brissotin orator, asserted in the Assembly that the defeats in Belgium had been caused by the betrayal of the French war plans—an allegation which was not, in fact, wide of the mark. At the same time, reports came in from the provinces of the renewal of the intrigues of the refractory priests. At the end of May and the beginning of June, the Assembly passed three decrees designed to meet the accumulating dangers of counter-revolution. On 27 May the departmental authorities were empowered to deport refractory priests who were denounced by twenty 'active' citizens. Those guilty of provoking civil disturbances were made liable to the same penalty on the testimony of a single 'active' citizen. On 29 May the Assembly passed a decree dismissing the 6,000 members of the King's guard, provided for under the Constitution. On 8 June a further decree summoned to the capital for the annual celebration of the fall of the Bastille 20,000 *fédérés* —or provincial National Guards. The last measure, carried on the initiative of the Minister of War, Servan, had two objects—to allow the regular troops garrisoned in Paris to be sent to the frontier, and to call into play in the capital an armed force, capable of neutralising the reactionary elements in the Parisian National Guard and the more radical of the sections.

Contrary to general expectations, Louis sanctioned the decree disbanding his constitutional guard, in the hope that, by continuing its pay secretly, he would, nevertheless, be assured of its loyalty. The decree for the establishment of a camp of *fédérés* outside Paris would, however, have left the king defenceless. Hoping for the arrival of the Austrian and Prussian troops, Louis decided to play for time by imposing his veto. In these tactics the king was encouraged by the staff officers of the Parisian National Guard, who promoted a petition to the Legislative Assembly on 10 June, calling for the decree to be rescinded. The effect of this demonstration, known as the petition of the 8,000, was offset the same day by the publication of a letter to the king from the Minister of the Interior, Roland, condemning the use of the veto. Taking advantage of the disagreement between Servan and Dumouriez, and stung by the provocative tone of Roland's letter, Louis then dismissed the majority of his Brissotin ministers on 13 June and imposed his veto on the decree against the refractory priests and the decree summoning the *fédérés*. Shortly after, Dumouriez resigned in order to take up a military command with the army of the north. The new ministry was formed, for the most part, of members of the Feuillant party.

The king's dismissal of his Brissotin or Girondin ministers had the same effect as his dismissal of Necker in July 1789—it stimulated radical sentiment in Paris and gave the signal for a series of revolutionary *journées*. Popular discontent in the capital could, however, now be directed and controlled through the assemblies of the forty-eight *sections*, into which Paris had been divided for administrative purposes, since the summer of 1790. At this point, popular leaders had incited these sectional assemblies to petition for permission to meet daily, for the admission of 'passive' as well as 'active' citizens, and for a general distribution of pikes. The rise in the cost of living during the early summer, suspicion of the court, and fears of foreign invasion combined once more to raise the political temperature. The Girondins were, therefore, emboldened to retaliate for the dismissal of their ministers by throwing their weight behind a popular demonstration, which had been planned for 20 June, with the ostensible purpose of celebrating the anniversary of the Tennis Court Oath. The original arrangements had provided for the planting of a tree of liberty in the Tuileries gardens, but the suggestion was now made, whether by mob-leaders or by the Girondins is not clear, that the demonstrators should carry arms. This was illegal, for the privilege of bearing arms was still a prerogative of the National Guard. The department of Paris, staffed by men of Feuillant leanings, condemned the demonstration from the outset and the participants appear to have been drawn exclusively from the radical faubourgs of St Antoine, St Marceau and the Observatory. Robespierre, too, did not encourage the popular rising at this stage, as he could see that it would play into the hands of the Girondins and because he feared that if Louis were deprived of his veto, the Feuillants would be given the excuse to press for a revision of the constitution. The movement, therefore, fell into the hands of popular leaders like Santerre, brewer of the faubourg St Antoine, Rossignol, a jeweller's assistant, Legendre, the butcher and friend of Danton, and Claude Lazowski, a factory inspector and colleague of Roland.

Owing to the inactivity or complicity of the police authorities, and in particular of Pétion, the mayor, and Manuel, the *procureur-général* of the Commune, the demonstration was allowed to take place as planned, on 20 June. Early in the morning, about 8,000 people from the eastern quarters of the capital made their way first to the town hall and later to the Legislative Assembly. Most of them, as 'passive' citizens, carried pikes, instead of firearms and, as on 5 and 6 October 1789, they included many women. On the motion of the Girondins the crowd was eventually admitted to the Assembly, where petitions were presented against the dismissal of the ministry and the use of the royal veto. From the Assembly the mob passed to the Tuileries gardens, and soon effected an entrance into the palace after a show of resistance by the National Guards. Surrounded by the demonstrators, who were armed with scythes, pitchforks and pikes, Louis showed no signs of flinching. He humoured the crowd by donning a red cap of liberty and drinking to the health of the nation, but calmly refused to withdraw his veto. His ordeal lasted several hours, until the palace was finally cleared by the mayor, Pétion. For the moment, therefore, the popular movement appeared to have misfired and its immediate result was to provoke a reaction in favour of the king. A monster petition, drafted by Dupont de Nemours, protesting against the *journée*, secured 20,000 signatures. On 7 July Pétion and Manuel were dismissed from their posts by the department of Paris. But the setback only forced the Girondins in the Assembly into greater activity and on 23 June, under this renewed pressure, Louis agreed to the formation of a camp of *fédérés* at Soissons. In so doing, he virtually surrendered the ground he had so stubbornly defended by his use of the veto, for some of the volunteers, on their way to the frontier, would need to pass through the capital. In this situation, the Minister of the Interior abandoned all effort to prevent the formation of an armed camp near Paris.

On 2 July the Assembly authorised the *fédérés* from the provinces to attend the usual ceremonies marking the 14 July, on condition that they moved on to Soissons a few days later.

The festivities on 14 July passed off without incident. The day was turned into a popular triumph for Pétion, who had been restored to his mayoral functions by the Assembly on the day before. Meanwhile, an important decree had been carried on 11 July, proclaiming 'the fatherland in danger'. This proclamation, which was not subject to the exercise of the veto, called up for national service all Frenchmen capable of bearing arms. On the same day, the Commune of Paris ordered that all citizens who possessed pikes should be drafted into the National Guard, and on 1 August the Assembly gave its sanction to a general distribution of these weapons. In this way, the character of the National Guard was suddenly changed from middle-class conservatism to radical democracy. Another result of the proclamation of the national emergency was that the administrative authorities were authorised to hold daily sessions and that the call-up of men and requisitioning of arms was pushed forward energetically. It was inevitable, in such circumstances, that the distinction between 'active' and 'passive' citizenship would lose all its meaning and that the sectional assemblies of the capital would insist on the right to meet daily. This right was, in fact, recognised by the Assembly on 25 July. The sections already had the power of drafting common petitions and nominating commissioners to a central organisation meeting at the Hôtel de Ville. They were thus in a position to bring immediate pressure to bear upon the constituted authorities in the capital.

The crisis was brought to a head by the arrival of the *fédérés*. The volunteers threw their whole weight behind the political demands of their hosts the *sectionaires*. They quickly formed a central committee of forty-three members at the Jacobin club. From this was constituted a secret committee of five to take in hand the preparations for an insurrection against the monarchy. It was the *fédérés* who stayed on in Paris after 14 July, who first raised the demand for the destitution of Louis XVI. This was made in a petition dated 17 July, almost certainly drafted by Robespierre. A second petition, presented to the Assembly on 23 July, and emanating from the Cordelier club, called for the summons of a national convention. The final incident which precipitated the fall of the monarchy was the manifesto of the duke of Brunswick, commander-in-chief of the Austrian and Prussian forces, the terms of which became known in Paris on 28 July. This document, drawn up by Fersen and an *émigré* called de Limon, announced that the allied armies were invading France to suppress anarchy and to restore the king to his rightful place of authority. Any National Guards who offered resistance would be shot and their homes demolished. The manifesto also declared that, if the Tuileries were again invaded, or the slightest violence offered to the royal family, exemplary vengeance would be taken on the capital. The fact that the issue of the declaration had been predicted in conservative journals in Paris earlier in the month seemed to confirm the existence of a widespread counter-revolutionary plot. Two days after its publication the *fédérés* from Marseilles arrived in the capital and were quartered in the faubourg St Antoine. Paris now heard for the first time the martial and inspiring music of Rouget de Lisle's marching song of the army of the Rhine—brought by the volunteers from Marseilles and known to history as the 'Marseillaise'. A popular insurrection was now imminent.

8

FROM THE FALL OF THE MONARCHY TO
THE EXTENSION OF THE WAR WITH EUROPE

(i) *The dethronement of Louis XVI and its results*

The attack on the royal palace of the Tuileries on 10 August 1792, like its aftermath, the September prison massacres, was the result of popular fears and suspicions of counter-revolution at a moment of national emergency. After the rising of 20 June Lafayette had returned to Paris in the effort to induce the Legislative Assembly to suppress the Jacobin club. He was known to be in touch with the king and it was clear that he would welcome the opportunity of restoring order in the capital by a military *coup d'état*. Louis had, in fact, rejected these offers of assistance, but it was generally assumed that he had accepted them. Rumours were also current of the king's impending escape from the capital and, in this respect, popular suspicions were well founded—for both the Feuillants and Lafayette had made preparations for his flight to Rouen or Compiègne. Danton had been warned of the existence of royalist plots in Brittany,[1] and a similar movement in southern France had only recently collapsed at Jalès. The Girondins, also, were rightly suspected of complicity in last-minute manœuvres to save the monarchy. Instead of indicting Lafayette, as they had promised, the Girondins showed signs of wishing to proceed against Robespierre. Their repeated attacks on the tottering Feuillant ministry showed that the Girondins were intent on recapturing control of the executive. This aim they were now seeking to accomplish, not by means of a revolutionary *journée* as on 20 June, but through secret negotiations with the

1. This movement was led by the marquis de la Rouërie and had been timed to synchronise with the Prussian invasion.

court. For these reasons, the impression gained ground in Paris that the king had decided to concert measures against the Assembly and the sections, with the object of facilitating a foreign invasion and of seizing control of the capital before the arrival of the *émigrés*.[1] It seemed, therefore, that unless the sections and their allies, the *fédérés*, moved quickly, the chance of preventing the execution of these royalist plots would be lost.

On the night of 9 August delegates from the Parisian sections displaced the legal municipal authority at the Hôtel de Ville and formed an insurrectional Commune. It was on the orders issued by this body that the sections and the *fédérés* marched on the royal palace on the following day. A desperate effort to intervene was made by Roederer—the proctor of the department of Paris—acting in close association with the Girondins. In order, if possible, to save the Tuileries from destruction and to afford the Legislative Assembly some chance of controlling events, Roederer induced Louis and his family to seek refuge among the deputies. This gamble to avoid armed conflict and bloodshed failed because, at the crucial moment, when the armed mob had effected an entry into the precincts of the palace, its Swiss defenders fired on the insurrectionists. As on the occasion of the fall of the Bastille, the demonstrators were convinced that they had been made the victims of a trap and, once they had gained the upper hand, nothing could restrain their vengeance. The royal palace was set on fire and 600 of the Swiss guards massacred. In the afternoon, the insurgents found themselves masters of the capital, about ninety of them having been killed in the assault and close on 300 wounded.

The Legislative Assembly had thus lost control of the situation. Its authority had been weakened by its passive attitude during the crisis and by the fact that it was now a rump parliament, owing to the recent desertion of its moderate members. It was preserved because it was hoped, thereby, to induce the army commanders and the local authorities throughout France to acquiesce in the work of the insurrectional commune. In effect, a tacit political bargain was struck between the new Parisian municipality and the national representative body. The Assembly recognised the existence of the Commune and the latter did not openly oppose the temporary political dispositions made by the Assembly. The latter suspended

1. The funds of the civil list had been employed to recruit a para-military organisation in Paris, which was paid to discredit the Assembly. This could have been converted into a disciplined body of troops at a moment's notice.

the king from his functions, ordered that the decrees upon which Louis had imposed his veto should be put into operation, established a provisional executive council of six ministers, and, on the instance of the Commune, summoned a National Convention to be elected on the basis of universal manhood suffrage. The suspension of the king was the work of the Girondins, who thus saved the monarchy from immediate abolition and left the final decision to the Convention. The Commune, for its part, promised to respect the life of the king, but insisted that the royal family should be imprisoned, not in the Luxembourg, but in the Temple, where it could be more closely guarded.[1]

The compromise thus effected was, however, an uneasy one. Radical opinion in the sections rightly considered that the Girondins had gone back on their previous promises to press for the immediate overthrow of the monarchy. These views were confirmed when the Girondins introduced certain safeguards into the electoral arrangements for the Convention. Among these was the retention of the system of indirect election, which ensured that the new Assembly would consist predominantly of middle-class representatives. The Girondins were also successful, despite the opposition of Robespierre, in preventing former members of the Constituent and Legislative Assemblies from being excluded from the Convention. The effect of the proclamation of universal suffrage was thus, to some extent, stultified, and when the Convention met it was found that the new electoral arrangements had enabled the Girondins to secure a majority. Above all, however, the crisis had left confronting each other two rival authorities in the capital—the Legislative Assembly, which had given the impression that it had accepted the rising with regret, and the insurrectional Commune, the representative of the radical sections.

It was one of the ironies of their political destiny that the Girondin ex-ministers were restored to power, not as their supporters had hoped by an understanding with the court, but as the result of the formidable popular revolt, which they had sought to circumvent. The Feuillant ministry had collapsed immediately and its members were soon in hiding. The ministries of the Interior, of Finance and of War were filled by the recall of their previous occupants—Roland, Clavière and Servan. The other three posts were filled by election in the legislature. The Admiralty went to Monge, a distinguished

1. The comte de Provence had escaped from the Luxembourg on 21 June 1791 The Temple had formerly been occupied by the comte d'Artois.

mathematician, the inventor of descriptive geometry and the tutor of the future 'organiser of victory', Lazare Carnot. His immediate usefulness in the task of national defence was as a technical expert in the manufacture of cannon. The new Minister of Foreign Affairs was Lebrun, who had had a chequered career as a cleric, soldier and journalist. This ministerial poll, however, was headed by the Jacobin lawyer, Georges Jacques Danton—'the Mirabeau of the mob', as he was called by the counter-revolutionaries—who was given the office of Minister of Justice. Danton had been chosen for his useful contacts with the Commune, and because of his dominating position in the capital during the recent crisis. The Girondin ministers were, in fact, conscious of their need for a 'lightning-conductor', for their popularity with the *sans-culottes* had declined sharply as a result of their negative and tortuous policy on the eve of the revolt. Although the provisional executive council of ministers had at this time no official president, Danton was its effective head and soon became the driving force behind the conduct of national defence. He resigned office late in September in order to take up his seat in the Convention, but at the height of the Prussian invasion he was, as Michelet so finely said, 'the voice of the revolution and of France'. The new administration, however, was thought to be only a caretaker government, unpopular in Paris because of its Girondin associations and the nominee of a dying legislature.

Far more formidable powers were wielded by the new insurrectionary Commune. This body differed from the legal municipal authority, which it had displaced, in several respects. Its membership was twice as large. The sections, which had previously been represented by three delegates, were now given six representatives on the general council, which thus consisted of 288 members. The new general council also met daily, whereas its predecessor had only been convoked at rare intervals by the mayor to decide matters of the greatest moment. The result was that the sectional representatives were now consulted at every turn on the smallest matters of administration, as well as on large questions of national policy. The preponderance of this large assembly in the government of the capital also derived from the fact that the 'municipal council' of thirty-two elected officials, virtually ceased to function. One further result of the revolution of 10 August was that the department of Paris was completely overshadowed by the Commune, which also absorbed the administrative functions of the 'district'. More especially because of its control of the police and of the National Guard, now commanded by the brewer, Santerre, the Commune had far more effective means of shaping events in the capital than the national representative assembly. The power of the Commune also extended far beyond Paris for, during the national emergency, it dispatched commissioners both to the provinces and to the armies. The members of this institution belonged, for the most part, to the lower middle class of small shopkeepers and artisans, though the liberal professions were also represented. Jaurès was undoubtedly incorrect in describing it as a 'proletarian' assembly—for it contained only two workmen, but its political views were, nevertheless, those of the *sans-culottes* of the sections.

The dethronement of Louis XVI was, in fact, a victory above all else for the direct democracy of the Parisian sections. Since July their general assemblies had been in permanent session and 'passive' as well as 'active' citizens were taking part in their discussions. In September the sections gained in cohesion and strength as a result of the reorganisation of the National Guard. Henceforward each of the forty-eight sections had its own battalion of the National Guard, whose movements and actions it could direct. In the new political situation created by the successful insurrection the sections, jealous of their own powers and independence, were able to play off the Legislative Assembly against the Commune or side with the Commune against the Assembly, as best suited their interests. The mood of the moment was reflected in their change of nomenclature— *Théâtre Français*, the home of Danton and the Cordelier club, became the section of *Marseilles*, *Place-Royale* the section *des Fédérés*, *Place Vendôme—les Piques*. Thus each of the old electoral wards of the capital was now an active political club and an autonomous segment of the larger Commune.

This shift in political power in the capital was accompanied by profound social and economic changes, which were forced on the National Assembly by the concerted pressure of the sections and of the Commune. On 26 and 28 August, the feudal landed dues (*droits réels*), which had survived the reforms of the Constituent Assembly, were abolished, except where the original deed conceding the tenancy could be produced. All common lands were declared to be the exclusive property of the village communities and the alienation of the lands of the *émigrés* in small lots was declared in principle. On 10 September the land laws were changed by the abolition of entail. In this way the Parisian *sans-culottes* endeavoured to make sure of the support of the rural population in the provinces. Finally, on 20

September, the registration of births, deaths and marriages was made the responsibility of the municipal authorities instead of the constitutional clergy, and legislation was also introduced instituting divorce.

(ii) *The September massacres*

Meanwhile, it remained to avenge the patriot 'victims' of the attack on the Tuileries, to track down those implicated in the royalist conspiracies and to put out of harm's way ecclesiastical fifth column-ists. After the desertion of Lafayette to the Austrians on 17 August a purge of the army commanders also became urgent. The problem of internal security was dealt with first. On 10 August the Vigilance Committee of the Legislative Assembly took to itself the power of ordering arrests and of ordering house to house searches. On the following day the prosecution of political crimes was transferred from the courts to the local administrative authorities, thus depriving those found guilty of the chance of appeal. Municipal bodies were thus empowered to make security regulations and to imprison offenders for a year, subject to the approval of the departmental authorities. In Paris the latter provision did not operate, so that the effect of the decree was to make the Commune the final authority for all matters of internal security. This was the origin of its vigil-ance committee—soon to acquire so sinister a reputation in Sep-tember. Normally, however, this responsibility was delegated to the sections, which in turn set up their own vigilance committees to interrogate and arrest suspected persons. In order to interrupt communications between counter-revolutionaries and to prevent the escape of suspects, the Commune suspended all internal passports on 12 August and several times closed the barriers of the capital. To acquire a passport it now became necessary to produce an identity card, or *certificat de civisme*, granted after careful scrutiny by the sectional vigilance committees. Between 10 August and the end of the month about 520 persons were arrested in Paris, of whom a half were refractory priests. Under the terms of a law carried on 26 August the latter should have been deported, but in Paris the demand for passports was so great that the priests were kept in prison and so became the chief victims of the September massacres. Persons accused of crimes against the state had so far been tried before the High Court at Orléans, but as this tribunal had been notoriously lenient in its sentences, the Legislative Assembly yielded to pressure from the Commune and established a 'revolutionary tribunal' for this purpose on 17 August. The machinery of what French historians call the 'First Terror' had thus been hastily improvised and was hardly functioning effectively when the traitorous capitulation of the frontier fortress of Longwy to the Prussians on 23 August led to an explosion of popular fury in Paris, which culminated in the September massacres.

The receipt of this disquieting news in Paris on 26 August led the Commune, at the instigation of Danton, to authorise house to house searches in the capital in order to deprive suspects of their weapons and to arm the volunteers. The search went on for two days, from 29 to 31 August, during which time all inhabitants of the city were confined to their homes, the shops were closed and military detachments from the sections were posted at every street corner. The results of the operation were disappointing, for only about 2,000 fire-arms were requisitioned, instead of the 80,000 which Danton had predicted. The search had also helped to spread alarm and consternation. Meanwhile the Assembly had decided to raise an immediate levy of 30,000 men in Paris and the neighbouring departments had issued a proclamation to the nation. Even Roland, who wished the Government to evacuate Paris, issued on 27 August a stirring circular to the frontier provinces, which presents a striking analogy in its phraseology with Churchill's invasion speeches of 1940.

'Let every town and every hamlet,' he said, 'man its defences, surround itself with ditches and entrenchments and prepare for a vigorous resistance. Watch the river-crossings and dispose yourselves so as to guard the bridges and highroads. Sow the path of the enemy with obstructions and see to it that he has to contend not only with those obstacles, but with the valour of the people and the army. The French people will know that if it flinches before these barbarians, it can expect from them, not merely the loss of its liberty, but the most cruel and long premeditated vengeance. Every means of salvation is justified at the height of the emergency. Nothing must be spared to save the fatherland.'

To this reminder of the threats contained in the Brunswick manifesto there were soon added bloodthirsty exhortations from the pen of the journalist Fréron.

Apart from the tense atmosphere thus generated in the capital, the rapidly deteriorating military situation on the eastern frontier and a fresh outbreak of conservative revolt in La Vendée, two other circumstances must be borne in mind if the ensuing massacres in the streets of Paris are to be understood. The first was the rumoured existence of a prison plot. At this time, the prisons in the capital were overcrowded, badly guarded and subject to periodical outbreaks.[1] The warders were corrupt, the prisoners could communicate easily between themselves and with the outside world. Mass escapes were frequent and the prisons were also notorious centres for the manufacture of false *assignats*. It was therefore hardly surprising that the popular imagination should have conjured up the spectre of an impending counter-revolutionary coup, for which the shock troops would be provided by throwing open the prisons. The opportunity for an outbreak would, it was thought, be afforded by the call-up of the *fédérés* and of the National Guards to the front. In these circumstances, the volunteers began to clamour for security for the lives and property of their dependants before they left the capital. In this sense the prison massacres were an example of popular 'preventive' justice.

The other circumstance is important because it helps to explain the paralysis of the established authorities in Paris on 2 September, at the moment when the massacres commenced. This was the attempt of the Girondins in the Legislative Assembly, on 30 August, to disband the insurrectionary Commune on the ground that it was exceeding its powers. On the motion of Roland, who was jealous of Danton's preponderance in the provisional executive committee, the Assembly decided to re-establish the legal Commune by calling for the election of a fresh 'general council' by the sections. Though this decision was rescinded on the afternoon of 2 September, this open conflict between the Assembly and the Commune added to the prevailing confusion and uncertainty and made effective action to repress the massacres impossible.

On the night of 1 September news arrived in Paris of the imminent fall of Verdun. On the following morning the Commune called on the citizens to arm themselves, closed the barriers and ordered the volunteers to assemble in the Champ de Mars. At midday Danton made an inspired speech in the Assembly calling on the country to save itself by its own courage and heroism. It was a fine Sunday, the crowds were out of doors and at two o'clock the alarm cannon was fired and the tocsin sounded from the church bells. At four

1. The main prisons in Paris were Bicêtre and La Salpêtrière (houses of correction for men and women respectively), Sainte-Pélagie (for debtors), Les Bernadins (for those condemned to the galleys), La Grande Force and La Petite Force (for men and women convicted of civil offences), L'Abbaye (for political offenders), La Conciergerie (for those awaiting trial at the Palais de Justice), Le Châtelet (for criminals), the Carmelite monastery and the seminary of St Firmin, where the refractory priests were held, and St Lazare (for prostitutes).

o'clock, just at the National Assembly adjourned, the massacres began. The first incident was an attack on a convoy of prisoners being taken in an open cart from the mayor's residence to the Abbaye prison. This was followed by an assault on the clergy imprisoned in the Carmelite monastery, some of whom were massacred in cold blood, and others after summary trial. Meanwhile, the Commune had met and had dispatched commissioners in the effort to save those imprisoned for civil offences and to advocate some form of popular trial for the rest. But neither the Commune, nor the National Assembly, did more than endeavour to limit the ferocity and extent of the massacres, and the murders were resumed in the evening at the Abbaye prison and soon spread to the Conciergerie, the Châtelet and La Force. On 3 September further massacres took place at the Abbaye and the slaughter spread to the seminary of St Firmin and the Bernadins. On the 4th members of the National Guard attacked Bicêtre prison and at La Force, the killing continued till the 7th. According to the latest estimates, those of M. Caron, about 1,200 persons were killed, or just under a half of the total prison population of Paris at the time. No less than 67 per cent of those who perished had been imprisoned on non-political charges. The explanation of this surprising fact is the popular fury against those who were supposed to be involved in the prison conspiracies, and the general resentment at the prison counterfeiters, whose activities were forcing up the cost of living.

There appears to be no reliable evidence that the massacres were systematically prepared or organised. The authorities in the capital were taken by surprise and were, no doubt, intimidated. Effective action to stop the massacres would have entailed the application of martial law, but repressive action of this sort had been discredited by the Champ de Mars incident of July 1791. Danton, as Minister of Justice, Roland, as Minister of the Interior, Santerre, as Commander of the National Guard, must all bear some of the responsibility. Danton's indifference to the fate of the prisoners may be attributed to his preoccupation with the problem of national defence, Roland was on the verge of physical collapse, and Santerre had not sufficient nerve or energy to see that his orders to the National Guard were enforced. No energetic action had been taken by the Legislative Assembly and the various attempts made to intervene by individual deputies saved a few lives but did not arrest the general slaughter. According to the latest evidence, it is probable that historians have, in the past, attributed too large a share of responsibility to the vigil-

ance committee of the Commune. This committee had been reconstituted on 2 September to include Marat, who had been urging the
elimination of the agents of counter-revolution, since 10 August and
even before. On 3 September the committee had issued, in the name
of the Commune, a circular to the departments inciting them to
follow the example of Paris, and it is almost certain that this had
been printed on Marat's own printing press. But the attribution of the
main responsibility for the massacres to the ten members of the
vigilance committee was an anti-Jacobin move, after the crisis, on the
part of the Girondins. The incriminated circular does not appear
to have had a wide distribution, or to have had much effect outside
Paris, and it is certain that the rôle and influence of Marat have been
exaggerated. It is impossible to place responsibility for the massacres
on an institution or a limited number of individuals. The tragedy
was directly due to the progress of the Prussian invasion and collective fears of an aristocratic plot in the capital. The massacres lasted
for several days partly because of the impotence of the constituted
authorities, and partly because the news from the frontier continued
to be bad. In that way the popular frenzy ran its course.

For a fortnight the situation remained critical, but even during
this period, a reaction set in against the massacres. The continuation
of the excesses alarmed the middle and propertied classes, and the
theft of the crown jewels on 17 September by criminals who had
escaped from the prisons, once more emphasised the helplessness of
the police authorities. Within a few weeks rival politicians in the
Convention were seeking to make political capital by attributing the
responsibility for the massacres to their opponents. The impression
created abroad by the prison slaughters was profound, and, especially
in Great Britain, robbed the revolutionaries of many of their early
friends and sympathisers.

(iii) *The Convention*

Meanwhile, at the end of August and beginning of September, the
primary and electoral assemblies had proceeded to the election of
members of the National Convention. Although the principle of
universal suffrage had been established, the outstanding fact about
the elections was their unrepresentative character. In certain departments only a quarter of those qualified to vote actually did so. These
abstentions may be attributed to general illiteracy or indifference,
and to the fact that the constitutional monarchists had been intimidated. Others had been excluded from the electoral assemblies

because they had refused to take the new civic oath to liberty and equality prescribed on 14 August. In Paris all those who had belonged to the Feuillant club, or who had subscribed the petitions of the 8,000 and 20,000 in June 1792, had been deprived of the franchise. Moreover, the electoral assembly of Paris had been transferred to the Jacobin club and the voting had taken place in public at the height of the massacres. Robespierre had also persuaded the Commune to allow the list of deputies elected for the capital to be revised by the sectional and primary assemblies. The result was that, with one exception, the twenty-four representatives of the capital were all Jacobins. Among these were men like Robespierre, Danton, Collot d'Herbois, Billaud-Varenne, Marat, Camille Desmoulins and the duke of Orléans, renamed Philippe Egalité—all supporters of the Commune. In the rest of the country, however, the Girondins were better known than their political opponents and were still regarded as devoted to the cause of national defence and the preservation of order. Some of the commissioners of the Commune, such as Momoro, had antagonised the provinces by putting forward suggestions for land nationalisation and had thus allowed the Girondins to rally the support of those who were afraid that confiscation would follow political equality and of all those who condemned the popular excesses in Paris.

The Convention assembled in the palace of the Tuileries on 20 September, just at the moment when Dumouriez and Kellermann had won the decisive artillery duel of Valmy in the Argonne against the Prussians. Its first act was to abolish the monarchy on 21 September, and to decree that the first year of the French republic should be dated from 22 September. So far, unity had prevailed, but the divisions among the members of the Convention soon came to the surface and rent the Assembly. As in the Legislative Assembly, the majority of the deputies—380 out of a total of 750—were drawn from local administrative bodies. Ninety-six ex-Constituents and 190 former members of the Legislative Assembly found seats in the Convention and the rest were newcomers.

(iv) *Girondins and Montagnards*

The political history of the Convention has been traditionally, and perhaps unjustifiably, identified with the duel between the Girondins and Montagnards.[1] Such an approach distracts attention from the great constructive reforms of the Assembly, especially in the

1. See M. J. Sydenham, *The Girondins*, London, 1961.

sphere of legal codification and educational progress. It does, however, direct attention to the primary importance of the Jacobin
achievement in the way of national defence, and to the social and
economic problems, which continued to perplex and divide the
revolutionaries. Many of the leading issues of the time were, in fact,
converted into 'party' issues and the conflict affords a convenient
thread through the complex and thronging events of the period.

In that struggle the Girondins had considerable initial advantages.
They had a majority in the Convention and a virtual monopoly of
the ministerial posts. Most of the Parisian newspapers—Brissot's
Patriote français, Louvet's *Sentinelle*, Gorsas' *Courrier des 83
départements* and Condorcet's *Chronique de Paris*—were controlled
by them and they could count on strong political support from the
provinces. As the group which had been identified with an aggressive
war policy, they stood to benefit politically from the sudden improvement in the country's military fortunes after Valmy. As moderates, they might also hope to benefit from the reaction against the
policy of repressive terror. Their political opponents in the Commune
had been discredited by the September massacres. The National Convention, recently elected and endowed with a mandate to endow
France with a new Constitution, seemed likely to afford the Girondins a much stronger buttress against the insurrectionary municipality than the rump of the old Legislative Assembly.

These advantages were frittered away by the Girondins in the
winter of 1792–3. They could, indeed, have only been preserved on
certain conditions, which called for the display of real statesmanship.
Marat's reference to the Girondins as '*hommes d'état*' was meant to
draw attention to the quality they most conspicuously lacked. In the
first place, if the Girondins were to make secure their claims to
continued power in the new situation, they should have seen the
primary necessity to combine political restraint on the home front
with a vigorous conduct of the war. In the second place, the Girondins should carefully have avoided any emphasis on the difference of
political and social outlook which had manifested itself in the elections between the capital and the provinces. And, finally, the Girondins should have realised that, inside the Convention, their political
fortunes would be dependent upon their gaining and retaining the
support of the independent members of the centre or 'Plain'. All the
subsequent misfortunes of the Girondins may be explained in terms
of their failure to appreciate these fundamental principles which
should have governed their conduct.

The differences which divided the Jacobins and Girondins were mainly the result of the personal rivalries of their respective leaders and of their divergent views on the relative political importance of the capital. From the outset, the Girondins indulged in violent campaigns of personal abuse against Robespierre, Marat and Danton, accusing them of wishing to erect a dictatorial triumvirate and failing to profit from the differences between Robespierre and Danton and the isolated position of Marat. The chief blame for this mistake rests with Roland, who was consumed with jealousy of Danton and with Madame Roland, who had become alienated from Robespierre. Even more serious, however, was the decision of the Gironde to continue its warfare against the insurrectionary Commune and to attempt to discredit Paris in the provinces. To some extent, this action is intelligible, in view of the necessity to preserve the security and independence of the Convention in a position bordering on anarchy. Nevertheless, the demands made in the last days of September by Roland and Buzot for the formation of a departmental guard to protect the Assembly gave a handle to their enemies in Paris. It enabled the Jacobins to accuse the Girondins of the crime of 'federalism', at a time when the republic had been proclaimed 'one and indivisible'. The charge was, in 1792 at least, unjustified, for no formal proposal was ever made by the Girondins for the transformation of France into a federal republic. Lasource's view, however, expressed on 25 September, that Paris should not have more political influence than that exercised by a single department, aptly summarised the opinion of the Girondins and can only be described as highly injudicious. Tactically, also, it was a mistake. Instead of taking advantage of the reaction against the massacres in several of the sections, the Girondins assailed the capital as a whole and thus turned against themselves the hostility of the Parisians as a community.

Equally misjudged was Roland's attack on Danton, who held a commanding political position as the chief intermediary between the Convention and the Commune and as virtual leader of the 'Plain'. Every consideration of political expediency and common sense should have led the Girondins to seek an understanding with the man who could have identified their cause with national resistance to the foreign invasion and have brought over to them much needed allies among the *sectionaires*. Instead Roland saw fit, when Danton retired from the Ministry of Justice at the end of September, to assail his financial integrity. Danton might have saved the Gironde and, on several occasions later, offered his collaboration—but his advances were rejected. Similarly, Louvet's celebrated attack on Robespierre at the end of October recoiled upon the Girondins, for the latter successfully defended himself before the Assembly in a powerful speech on 5 November, which did much to discredit his opponents. When, moreover, Vergniaud attempted to saddle the Jacobins with the responsibility for the September massacres, all prospects of reconciliation faded.

(v) *The King's trial and execution*

The first decision of high political significance taken by the Convention, after the abolition of the monarchy, was the trial of Louis XVI. The debate on this issue brought into the full glare of public attention the mutual suspicions and antagonisms of the rival political groups. Ever since 10 August the king's trial seemed probable. Louis' treason in the months before the insurrection seemed to have been established, and so long as the danger of a recrudescence of the massacres existed, his safety in the Temple remained doubtful. The issue had first been raised at the end of August in the Jacobin club by the journalists Hébert and Fréron. The matter, however, bristled with difficulties. The king's defenders argued that Louis was inviolable, unless he could be proved to have broken his oath to the constitution, or to have resorted to flight, or to have placed himself at the head of an army in order to overturn the constitution. He had, in fact, committed one of these offences by his escape to Varennes, but it was contended that the restitution of his powers by the Legislative Assembly had amounted to an amnesty. The punishment prescribed—dethronement—had already been carried into effect, and it was therefore argued that no act committed before 10 August could be made the subject of a further indictment. This, however, was to base the king's defence upon a political situation which had ceased to exist, for the 10 August had put an end to the Constitution of 1791. It also seemed to throw doubt on the validity of the popular insurrection. The republicans, on the other hand, contended that Louis could and should be held responsible for his overt acts of counter-revolutionary intrigue. Whether he should be subjected to trial was arguable. In Robespierre's view, there was no need for a trial, since the king had already been condemned by the revolution of 10 August. To try Louis, Robespierre argued, would merely be to appeal from the verdict of the sovereign people to that of a judicial tribunal. On this contention, the only matter for consideration was Louis's punishment.

The Convention did not rebut this line of argument, but rejected it in favour of a trial. It was considered dangerous to condemn the king without giving him a hearing and the proofs of his treason were, after the discovery of the iron chest in the Tuileries on 20 November, readily available. But, by deciding to try Louis itself, the Convention could hardly escape the criticism that it was presuming to act both as prosecutor and judge. There was the further issue of what the sentence should be, if Louis was found guilty. Here, again, the view of Robespierre was unambiguous. There could, he contended, be only one punishment, the death penalty. Such a decision, however, would not only make Louis a martyr, it would also antagonise the courts of Europe and involve the danger of an extension of the war. These considerations made many moderates, including Danton, hesitate to apply this extreme measure.

The whole issue was, therefore, an extremely complicated one and eminently suited to emphasise the political antagonisms between the Jacobins and Girondins. For various reasons, the Gironde eventually decided to try and avoid a judicial trial, or, if that proved impossible, to spare Louis capital punishment, if pronounced guilty. Such a course of action involved political manœuvres which it was easy to condemn as counter-revolutionary. The final expedient devised by the Girondins to save Louis was to suggest that the question of Louis' punishment should be made subject to ratification by the country at large. This seemed to be taking a page out of the Jacobins' book by appealing to direct democracy, but it was condemned by the enemies of the Gironde as an expedient for resorting to political federalism. In the event, a unanimous verdict of guilty was returned against the king and Louis was condemned to death by 387 votes to 334. As twenty-six of the majority had been in favour of an amendment for suspending the death sentence, a fresh vote was taken on the deferment of execution and the final decision to execute Louis was taken by a majority of seventy. Louis was guillotined on 21 January 1793.

(vi) War with Europe

Valmy had been a great defensive victory but, by saving France, it enabled the republican armies to go over to the offensive and the Girondins to pursue their projects of ideological warfare against European despots. In the month which followed (21 September–21 October) French armies occupied two possessions of the crown of Sardinia—Savoy and Nice. In the north-east, Custine was success-

ful in obtaining control of the left bank of the Rhine as far as
Mayence. Meanwhile, the Austrians, under the duke of Saxe-
Teschen, had held Lille in close siege from 27 September to 7 October.
The heroic defence of the town against repeated bombardment
finally discouraged the Austrians, who then retreated to Belgium.
After Valmy, the Prussians had conducted an inglorious withdrawal,
negotiating *en route* with Dumouriez and thinking in terms rather
of partitioning Poland in the east than France in the west. This set
Dumouriez free to take up the pursuit of the Austrians and to enter
Belgium. On 6 November he won a decisive victory against the
Austrians at Jemappes, which placed the country at his mercy.

The effect of these successes on the Convention in November and
December was to cause it to adopt, on the initiative mainly of the
Gironde, a series of decrees which made the extension of the conflict
inevitable. On 16 November the provisional executive council,
acting as if Belgium was already French property, opened the Scheldt
estuary to the shipping of all nations, thus repudiating the provisions
of the Treaty of Münster of 1648, which had guaranteed the exclusive
navigation of that river to the Dutch. The breach of this international
guarantee not only indicated the revolutionary contempt for the
public law of Europe, and seriously antagonised Great Britain, it
also indicated that Dumouriez's plans for the conquest of Holland
were maturing. On 19 November the ideological warfare was continued by a decree offering 'fraternity and assistance' to all peoples
wishing, like the French, to recover their liberty. On 27 November the
Convention, yielding to the local aspirations for union with France,
annexed Savoy. France had now unmistakably thrown overboard
all her previous professions of non-aggression. This policy was driven
home by an important decree of 15 December, carried on the motion
of Cambon. It was announced that French occupation would be
followed by the sequestration of noble and ecclesiastical property,
the introduction of French paper currency and the destruction of
feudal dues and obligations. Notice was thus served on Europe that
conquest would be made to pay its own way and that revolutionary
social doctrines would be applied wherever the French armies penetrated. Despite the protests of Dumouriez, this decree was rigorously
applied to Belgium in January 1793 and it alienated whatever sympathies for the revolution the inhabitants had hitherto possessed.
In this way, annexation became not only desirable, but necessary.
On 31 January Danton, in advocating the annexation of Belgium,
enunciated the doctrine of 'natural frontiers', according to which the

republic could legitimately expand its boundaries to the Rhine and the Alps. On the same day orders were given to Dumouriez to occupy Holland. Such action was bound to bring Great Britain into the war with revolutionary France. Since the execution of Louis, Anglo-French diplomatic relations had been broken off and on 1 February 1793, the Convention, anticipating the inevitable, declared war on Britain. By March, France was at war with most of Europe, with the exception of Russia and one or two Scandinavian powers.[1]

1. The decrees of 16 November 1792 and 31 January 1793 were both 'provoked' by developments outside France. The opening of the Scheldt was designed to wean the commercial interests in Antwerp from supporting the conservative faction in Belgian politics, while the doctrine of 'natural frontiers' was invented largely in response to petitions from the Rhineland in favour of annexation by France.

9

THE RISE OF REVOLUTIONARY GOVERNMENT
AND THE CRISIS OF NATIONAL DEFENCE

(i) *Military and economic difficulties* (*January–March 1793*)

Despite Pitt's difficulties in constructing the first coalition and the allies' lack of a concerted strategy, France soon found that the war with Europe posed new and more serious problems of national defence. The Girondins had planned to speed executive decisions by the establishment, on 1 January 1793, of a Committee of General Defence, but this body was too numerous for its policy to be kept secret, and was only endowed with limited powers of controlling the ministers. The resignation of Roland on 22 January and the capture by the Jacobins of the Committee of General Security after the assassination of the Conventionnel Lepelletier, left the Girondins in a weaker position on the home front. Garat, who took Roland's place at the Ministry of the Interior, was a trimmer who avoided binding political commitments. In February, the Girondins still held the key ministries of Finance, War and Foreign Affairs, but Clavière, Beurnonville and Lebrun were unpopular with the *sans-culottes*, and were increasingly attacked in the Convention on account of their connexions with the war contractors. The problem of raising the more numerous armies, which were now urgently required, continued to perplex the administrators. On 25 January Dubois-Crancé had once more stressed the necessity of amalgamating the volunteers and the regular infantry, and had pleaded for the mobilisation of a further 300,000 men. The fusion of the National Guard with the troops of the line, however, involved years of administrative effort before it was completed and the levy of 300,000, decreed by the Convention on 23 February, rekindled in the west of France all the old antagonism to military service which had existed before 1789.

The general war also created serious financial and economic difficulties. It was found impossible to meet the increased war expenditure except by inflationary methods and, in the spring of 1793, the circulation of the *assignats* was substantially increased. Pitt soon showed that he had no scruples in the waging of economic warfare, the principles and practice of which had been perfected in the Seven Years' War. Using British and foreign bankers in Paris, particularly the firm of Boyd and Kerr, he undertook measures to turn the foreign exchanges against France, allowed royalists, after 1793, to manufacture counterfeit *assignats* in England and subjected French commerce to an ever-tightening economic blockade. The Convention itself contributed to French economic isolation by repudiating the Anglo-French commercial treaty of 1786, and by abandoning the principle of 'the freedom of the seas'. Except through Switzerland and Geneva, the French were cut off from economic contact with Europe, while the British fleet resumed the maritime and colonial operations, which had proved so successful throughout the eighteenth century. These factors caused the rapid depreciation of the French paper currency. By February 1793 the purchasing power of the *assignats* had dropped to 50 per cent of their nominal value and the prices of articles of general consumption had risen sharply. In the same month there was an acute shortage of coffee, soap and sugar and, shortly afterwards, the familiar signs of a bread scarcity in the capital were apparent. All efforts to mitigate the shortages by importing grain from abroad, particularly from Genoa and America, and by subsidising the price of bread in Paris were unavailing.

(ii) *Sectional movements in Paris* (*February–April 1793*)

The consequent social and economic discontent in the capital was, as always, stimulated and canalised by popular demagogues. The most active of these, in the spring of 1793, were Jacques Roux, a priest, and Varlet, an *employé* in the postal services. Adopting the popular demands for the fixing of food prices, for the requisitioning of food supplies and for measures to check the activities of the corn monopolists, these radical leaders built up for themselves powerful support in the sections and the *banlieue* of Paris. As the Girondins made no secret of their objections to the principles of a controlled economy, and as they were generally suspected of close contacts with the class of war profiteers, they soon incurred the hostility

of the new radical movement, which gathered strength as the
economic and military situation deteriorated. At the end of February
and beginning of March a series of insurrectionary *journées* in the
capital, organised by the extremists or *Enragés*, pointed to the growing seriousness of the class conflict and to the political isolation of
the Girondins. The most important of these sectional movements
occurred on 10 March, after news had been received that Coburg,
the Austrian commander, had outmanœuvred Dumouriez, had
occupied Liège and had crossed the Meuse. The situation recalled
the dangers that had precipitated the September massacres. Danton,
who again rallied the country to fresh efforts against the coalition,
pressed for the establishment of a revolutionary tribunal to prevent
the popular fury against fifth columnists from getting out of control.
The insurrection, however, failed to secure the backing either of the
Commune or of the Jacobin club and collapsed. The crisis was hardly
over when the department of La Vendée revolted against the levy of
300,000 men and, between 10 and 15 March, the peasants of the
west, who had been alienated by the rigorous measures taken against
the refractory priests, rose *en masse* under the leadership of Stofflet,
Cathelineau, d'Elbée and La Rochejaquelin. The only forces
available for the repression of the revolt consisted of raw recruits
and National Guards, but the rebels were unskilled except in guerilla
warfare and were content with local successes.[1] The March crisis had
a permanent significance in the history of the revolution, because it
gave birth to several institutions, which helped to save the country
at the hour of its greatest need, but which later became identified
with the Terror. On 9 March, when it had become evident that the
military levy was provoking regional resistance, the Convention
decided to dispatch eighty of its members, endowed with full
powers, to the provinces with orders, at all costs, to break the
opposition. The official designation of these agents of the central
government was 'Commissioners of the Convention', but they became famous as '*représentants en mission*'. There was a close connexion between the dispatch of these commissioners and the re-institution
on 10 March of the Revolutionary Tribunal for the summary trial
of those accused of crimes against the state, since the deputies were
unwilling to leave the capital until this measure of security had been
carried. The Girondins seized their opportunity to nominate Jacobins
as commissioners in order to increase their own majority in the

1. For recent sociological reinterpretations of the Vendéen risings see P. Bois, *Les
paysans de L' Ouest*, Le Mans, 1960, and C. Tilly, *The Vendée*, London, 1964.

Convention, but in doing so enabled their opponents to recruit much political support in the departments. On 19 March, the Convention carried a decree, introduced by Cambacérès, creating military commissions of five members with powers to execute within twenty-four hours rebels who were captured under arms. The same law outlawed all those accused of complicity in revolts against the levy. A further repressive measure was a decree of 21 March which provided for the election in each section or commune of a 'revolutionary committee' of twelve members, consisting of *sans-culottes* who were entrusted with the duty of rounding up foreigners and political 'suspects' without passports. Finally, on 28 March, the laws against the *émigrés* were codified and all proved *émigrés* were made subject to the pains and penalties of civil death.[1]

Nothing, however, was done to concede the demands of the *Enragés*, with the result that the sectional unrest in the capital continued and this found a new source of strength in a central representative committee, which took to meeting in the archbishop's palace. One of the aims of this committee was the promotion of closer relations between the capital and the provinces, and on 2 April the Commune of Paris itself established a corresponding committee, hoping thereby to offset the Girondin schemes for a federation of the conservative departmental authorities by a Jacobin federation of communes.

(iii) *The fall of the Gironde* (*5 April–2 June 1793*)

Meanwhile, the news from the front gave increasing cause for anxiety. In Belgium, despite the protests of Dumouriez, French agents had provoked general unrest by putting the decree of 15 December 1792, into operation, confiscating public funds and the property of the church. Dumouriez returned to Brussels to put a stop to these activities and, on 12 March, sent a letter of violent recrimination to the Convention. Danton was dispatched to Belgium but failed to reach an understanding with the general, whose counter-revolutionary sympathies were reinforced by further military reverses. His troops were beaten on 18 March at Neerwinden and on 21 March at Louvain. Shortly afterwards, he concluded an armistice with the Austrians and made preparations for returning to the capital to restore the monarchy in the person of Louis XVII and to reimpose the

1. All Frenchmen who had left the country after 1 July 1789, and had not returned before 9 May 1792, and those who could not prove continuous residence after the latter date, were now regarded as *émigrés* and banished.

constitution of 1791. When the Convention dispatched the War
Minister, Beurnonville, and four deputies to relieve him of his command at the end of March, Dumouriez handed them over to the
Austrians. After he had failed to induce his troops to support the
projected *coup d'état* in Paris, the general and several members of
his staff deserted to the enemy on 5 April. Dumouriez had been so
closely identified with Girondin policy both as a minister and as a
general that his former political associates in the Convention found
it difficult to repudiate the charge of complicity in his treason. Their
attempt to forestall this attack on 2 April by accusing the Jacobins of
attempts to intrigue with Dumouriez through the friends and relations of Philippe Egalité (former duke of Orléans) recoiled on their
heads, since its only result was finally to alienate Danton.

The effect of these disasters in Paris was twofold. On the one hand,
Danton's case for the strengthening of the executive government
now proved irresistible and, on the other, the agitation in the
sections for the expulsion of the Girondin leaders from the Convention could also employ the argument of the military necessity. On
6 April the Committee of General Defence was transformed into
the Committee of Public Safety. The members of this first Committee
of Public Safety, which may be regarded as Danton's second
administration, consisted of Barère, Delmas, Bréard, Cambon,
Danton, Robert Lindet, Guyton-Morveau, Treilhard and Delacroix.
Though events had thus, at last, demolished the former theoretical
objections to allowing members of the legislature to exercise executive
functions, the committee was, at this stage, specifically denied the
power to issue arrest warrants and to exercise any independent control over finance. Nevertheless, it was, to all intents and purposes, the
first French cabinet in the modern sense and during the course of
the summer gradually absorbed more and more power to itself.
Effective machinery for the higher direction and control of the war
effort had thus come into being. The attack on the Girondins as
the alleged accomplices of Dumouriez had been started by Robespierre, but this lead was quickly followed by the radical sections.
On 8 April the section of *Bon Conseil* sent a deputation to the Convention to demand a strict inquiry into the circumstances of Dumouriez's treason and called on the Jacobin deputies to 'wage a war to
the death on the moderates'. On 10 April the *Halle au Blé* section
promoted an address to the Convention not only denouncing the
Girondins but demanding their arrest and the execution of Roland.
The Jacobins were summoned to save the republic, but at the same

time warned that if they did not feel equal to the task, the sections would take matters into their own hands. This threatening address shortly afterwards secured the backing of thirty-three of the forty-eight sections and, on 15 April, was adopted by the Commune. On the same day the address, which now demanded the expulsion of twenty-two Girondin leaders from the Convention, was read in the National Assembly by Alexandre Rousselin, a protégé of Danton. Though the Convention adjourned the discussion of this address and voted it a 'calumny' on 20 April, the political programme for the next revolutionary *journée* had thus been framed.

In the last resort, however, the Girondins dug their own political graves by a series of ill-judged blunders, and by a stubborn refusal to face economic and military facts. The first of these miscalculations was the decision on 13 April to bring Marat for trial before the Revolutionary Tribunal. The charge was that, as president of the Jacobin club, he had signed a circular of the Society on 5 April appealing for help against Dumouriez to the provincial patriots and denouncing as the general's accomplices deputies who had voted for the submission of the king's fate to a national referendum. By thus sponsoring a decree of accusation against a member of the Convention the Girondins set the dangerous precedent of tampering with the inviolability of members of the National Assembly. They had, moreover, attacked a popular favourite and brought him before a court whose verdict, in the circumstances, was a foregone conclusion. They were equally blind to the growing strength of the popular demand for the regulation of corn prices. On 18 April the municipal authorities of Paris had drawn up a petition at the Jacobin club in favour of the establishment of maximum prices for corn. When the Convention attempted to shelve the issue by referring the petition to its agricultural committee, the General Council of the Commune announced that it would be 'in a state of revolution' until the food problem had been solved. Popular pressure from the sections became so insistent that, on 4 May, the Convention was compelled to submit and to revert to the system of the governmental control of corn prices. This concession had been made by the Jacobins for political reasons and it paid immediate dividends by attracting the support of the *sans-culottes*.

Nevertheless, the ministers and the Committee of Public Safety became increasingly restive at the continued encroachments of the Commune and, on 18 May, Garat, as Minister of the Interior, brought forward proposals for the suppression of the municipality and the transfer of a newly formed Convention to Bourges. These suggestions were too drastic for the Committee of Public Safety and, as a compromise, Barère proposed the establishment of a Commission of Twelve to investigate the recent conduct on the Commune and sections. This commission was elected on 21 May and consisted almost entirely of Girondins. It eagerly seized the opportunity to carry the war into the enemy's camp by issuing orders, on 24 May, for the arrest and imprisonment of Hébert— the deputy proctor of the Commune, and of Varlet, by inducing the Convention to curtail the political activities of the sections, and by taking steps to reinforce the guards of the Legislative Assembly. These ill-judged measures raised a storm of opposition in the Commune and sections. The former demanded that Hébert should be restored to his functions and promptly judged, the latter that the Commission of Twelve should be dismissed for having exceeded its powers. When Dobsen, the president of the section of the *Cité*, refused to surrender his registers for examination by the Commission both he and the secretary of the section were also imprisoned. Under these provocations, the mob surrounded and burst its way into the Convention on 27 May and the Assembly was compelled to abolish the Commission of Twelve and to release the prisoners. Though the Girondins re-established the Commission on the following day, the prisoners remained at large and took a leading part in the insurrection which quickly followed.

Not only had the Girondins done their best to overthrow the Commune, they had also stimulated, in the course of May, a series of political revolts against the political dominance of the capital. Marseilles had defied the rule of the Convention since the beginning of the month and later overthrew its Jacobin municipal authority by a popular insurrection. On 21 May Bordeaux declared its intention of amassing sufficient armed strength to overawe the *sans-culottes* in the capital and the same plan was supported by several other moderate municipalities, such as Caen. The department of the Jura invited the other departmental authorities, in which Girondin influence was pronounced, to send supplementary delegates to form a new Convention at Bourges. The federalist revolt had, therefore, already attained serious proportions in the last days of May, and can be said to have been the final political mistake committed by the Gironde before it was overthrown.

On the night of 28 May a meeting of sectional representatives met at the bishop's palace and formed an insurrectional committee.

On 31 May this authority abolished the Commune, reconstituted it and sought to convert it into the submissive agent of the *sans-culottes*. Hanriot was designated as commander of the National Guard. The department of Paris came into line by appointing a commission, which threw in its lot with the insurrectionaries. The arrest of the Girondin leaders, measures against the 'suspects' entrusted to a 'revolutionary army', the extension of price controls to the whole range of articles of primary necessity, the purge of the army and civil service and the immediate raising of a forced loan to be levied on the rich—such were the demands now presented for fulfilment. There was, indeed, a real danger that the insurrectionary committee, in expelling the Girondin leaders, would put an end to the existence of the Convention itself. Both the Commune and department of Paris, despite their complicity with the sections, and even the Jacobin deputies themselves were, however, agreed on the necessity of avoiding such drastic action. On 31 May the petition of the sections for the arrest of the Girondins was referred to the Committee of Public Safety and the only concession made to the demonstrators was the abolition of the Commission of Twelve. After this initial rebuff, the insurrectionary committee completed its plans for intimidating the Convention on Sunday, 2 June. This time the Convention, surrounded by Hanriot's National Guard, submitted and placed twenty-nine of the Girondin deputies, together with the ministers Clavière and Lebrun, under house arrest.

Bloodshed and the dissolution of the Convention had thus been avoided, but the social and economic demands of the *sans-culottes* remained unsatisfied. It is true that, on 4 June, the principle of the 'revolutionary army' had been accepted, but the Convention made no effort to translate it into practice. Marat complained that the Committee of Public Safety had misjudged the popular revolt and the *Enragés* were bitter in their denunciation of the irresolute attitude of the established authorities. Meanwhile, the Girondins, bereft of their leaders, were quick to exploit the resentment felt by the deputies at the intimidation of the Assembly. On 5 June Boyer-Fonfrède demanded a report on the deputies who had been arrested and warned the Assembly of the impending arrival of the men from Bordeaux. Much sympathy was expressed with Madame Roland, who had been arrested by order of the insurrectionary committee, released and re-arrested. Several of the Girondins escaped from house arrest and others wrote letters to the departments inciting them to send addresses of reproval to the Convention. On 6 and 19 June

seventy-four Girondin deputies signed a collective and secret protest
against the Jacobin *coup d'état*, which soon became known to the
government. These men were later arrested and were only saved from
the revolutionary tribunal by the personal intervention of Robespierre.

The problem that faced the Committee of Public Safety after 2
June 1793, was, therefore, twofold. In the first place it was necessary
to get rid of, or at least to emasculate, the insurrectionary committee, if possible without permanently alienating the *sans-culottes* and,
in the second place, it was also urgent to prevent a reaction in favour
of the Girondins and, above all, to forestall a widespread federalist
revolt in the provinces.

(iv) *The Federalist revolt and the collapse of the first Committee of
Public Safety* (*May-July 1793*)

Fortunately, for the executive government, the insurrectionary
committee possessed no financial resources of its own and was,
moreover, composed of discordant political elements. The Committee had promised the *sans-culottes* who had been called out to
effect the insurrection of 31 May–2 June forty *sous* a day as compensation for their loss of wages. This bill had now to be honoured and
was presented for payment to the Committee of Public Safety. This
gave the government its chance to impose conditions, and the account
was settled on the understanding that the committee would be
dissolved. In fact, the department of Paris collaborated in this move
by summoning fresh delegates from the sections to form a new
committee under the style of 'committee of public safety of the
department of Paris', constituted on 8 June. From this new authority
all members of the *Enragés* were excluded, and its functions were
confined to administrative and police matters. The committee had
thus lost its insurrectionary character and become a cog in the regular
administrative machine of the capital.

The efforts to stifle the federalist revolt, however, were less successful. These took two forms—economic concessions to the peasants,
and the drawing up of a new constitution, designed to convince the
departments that the alleged danger of a Jacobin dictatorship was
unreal. On 3 June the Convention decided to alienate the estates
of the *émigrés* in small lots, in order to afford the poorer peasants
the chance of acquiring land individually. A week later permission
was granted to the village communities to divide up the common
fields and, in communes without common fields, poor peasants

were given the opportunity of renting *émigré* lands instead of buying them. Finally, on 17 July, all surviving seigneurial dues (*droits féodaux*) were abolished outright without compensation to the previous owners. These decrees marked the culmination of the attack on the feudal *régime*, which had been begun on 4 August 1789. Ultimately, they may be said to have satisfied the aspirations with which the peasants had entered on the revolution but, for the moment, they exercised no direct influence on the political situation, mainly because provincial discontent had arisen from the military levy.

The Jacobin constitution of 1793 was probably never intended to be put into operation. In essence, it was a political manœuvre, as is indicated by the haste with which the initial Girondin draft was revised by the Jacobin constitutional committee and approved by the Convention between the end of May and the 24 June. Its most significant features were the declaration of rights, which formed its prologue, and the provision for the institution of a popular referendum on legislation. The declaration now included among the rights of man the principles of freedom of worship and labour, and also made important contributions to the evolution of social theory and the conception of the welfare state. The purpose of society was declared to be the happiness of the people, public assistance the right of the infirm or unemployable, public education a general necessity. These advances registered and reflected the social theories of Robespierre. The constitution provided for the direct election of a national legislative assembly under a system of universal suffrage. The executive was to consist of a council of twenty-four, nominated by the legislature from lists of candidates indirectly elected. Legislative acts were divided into two categories—decrees and laws. The former were to go into force immediately, but the latter were made subject to a popular referendum. The referendum, however, under the conditions set out in the constitution, could hardly have been effective and the most vital tasks of maintaining internal security and providing for national defence could be carried out by means of decrees. In fact, the constitution would have been unworkable. Annual sessions of the Legislative Assembly would have condemned the country to continuing political turmoil, the executive would have been ineffective, and the arrangements for local government had been left undetermined. Nor should one be deceived by the overwhelming approval which the constitution received from the country at large, for many voted in its favour because they wished to get rid

of the Convention. Hence it is not surprising that, once the acceptance of the constitution had been officially celebrated at Paris on 10
August, it was deposited in a cedar box in the Convention and
forgotten by all, except those who wished to overturn the government. Even as a political manœuvre the constitution failed, for the
federalist revolt continued to make alarming progress during the
summer of 1793.

The federalism which was said by its enemies to have inspired
these scattered revolts against Jacobin domination in Paris was of a
thin and unsubstantial character. It owed something to Rousseau's
rejection of republican forms as unsuitable to large states, and to the
success of federalism in America, but essentially it reflected the
impatience of many provincial towns at the loss of their former
independence and social prestige. It is, however, doubtful whether
there existed any agreement among the leaders of these provincial
risings on the desirability of dividing the country into small independent republics united by a federal bond. Nevertheless, the majority of the departmental administrations of the time were still staffed
by men whose social connexions and political convictions robbed
them of any sympathy with the Jacobin idea of a republic 'one and
indivisible'. Most of them were believers in constitutional monarchy
and were as convinced, as their successors in 1848, that political
democracy would entail attacks on private property. The centres of
this provincial unrest were, in the north, Caen, in the centre, Lyons,
in the south, Toulouse, Bordeaux and Marseilles. As has already
been emphasised, the revolts had started at the end of May, but the
expulsion of the Gironde on 2 June gave a further impetus to the
risings. Twelve of the Girondin leaders, who had been placed under
house arrest, escaped from Paris and made their way to Normandy,
Brittany and the south calling on their sympathisers for armed support. Early in June, the risings spread from the Eure department to
Calvados, Finistère, Ille-et-Vilaine, Côtes-du-Nord, Morbihan and
Mayenne. In the south, Paoli raised Corsica, while Nîmes and Toulon imitated Bordeaux and Lyons in expelling the *représentants en
mission* and stamping out Jacobin influence. In the middle of June
sixty departments were in more or less open revolt.

Nevertheless, the federalist movement failed, and for obvious
reasons. It was discredited by its association with the royalists and
émigrés, it was badly led and, at the moment of greatest peril, the
activity and loyalty of the revolutionary committees of the communes proved more than a match for the tepid enthusiasm of the

recalcitrant departmental authorities. The renewed foreign invasion also did much to deter moderate political opinion from siding with the Girondins. And, finally, the initial conciliatory policy of the Committee of Public Safety towards the rebels and the economic concessions offered to the peasants after 2 June gradually bore fruit and helped to localise resistance.

Meanwhile, on 10 July, the Committee of Public Safety, which had been re-elected monthly without change, was overthrown. Seven of its fourteen members—Danton, Delacroix, Cambon, Delmas, Guyton-Morveau, Berlier and Ramel—were now eliminated. Two new members—Prieur de la Marne and Thuriot—were added and the total membership was thus reduced to nine. These changes had been effected as the result of accumulating criticism of the committee's conduct of the war and of Danton's foreign policy. The committee had, in fact, failed to stem the tide of French military reverses which had set in since Dumouriez had deserted. The Austrians had quickly invaded France, laid siege to the frontier fortresses of Condé and Valenciennes and forced the French army of the north back on defensive positions protected by the fortresses of Bouchain and Cambrai. The army of the Rhine under General Custine had also fallen back precipitately on Alsace, leaving Mayence to be surrounded by the Prussians on 14 April. If Cambrai fell the Austrians would be free to thrust towards Paris and if Mayence surrendered the Prussians could overrun Alsace and Lorraine. At the end of May Pitt concluded an offensive and defensive alliance with Spain and Spanish armies were soon threatening to invade France at both ends of the Pyrenees. Savoy, too, was endangered by Sardinian armies, though operations in this sphere did not begin till the middle of August.

To meet these dangers, the government had transferred Custine from the army of the Rhine to the command of the army of the north at the end of May. Custine's defensive strategy was to draw on the forces of the armies of the Rhine and the Moselle to strengthen his new armies, so as to ensure the relief of Condé and Valenciennes. His plans were based on the assumption that Mayence, which was well stocked with provisions, would be able to withstand a protracted siege. Unfortunately, on 9 June, the Vendéen rebels captured Saumur and panic quickly spread through the whole valley of the Loire. In this new situation the committee was obliged to transfer the troops of the army of the Rhine, which had been allocated to Custine, to the defence of the west. With his forces thus depleted, Custine

was compelled to remain inactive and, at the beginning of July, the fall
of Condé and Valenciennes became inevitable. Condé surrendered
on 10 July, Mayence on the 23rd and Valenciennes on the 28th.

The blame for these continuing disasters was placed partly upon
Custine, whose military plans had been violently criticised by the
radical War Minister, Bouchotte, and partly upon Danton, who
since April had been pursuing a foreign policy designed to appease
the hostile coalition. On 13 April Danton had induced the Convention to agree to a reversal of its previous foreign policy by announcing its intention not to interfere in the government of other powers.
In effect, the Convention had thus abrogated the decrees of 19
November and 15 December 1792, which had done so much to
antagonise Belgium and Great Britain. In consonance with this new
policy, Danton had set on foot negotiations both with the smaller
neutral powers, who had been France's traditional allies, and with
the enemy. Danton continued to hope that both Prussia and Great
Britain could be divided from Austria, and that the Austrians would
agree to surrender the ex-minister Beurnonville in exchange for
Marie Antoinette. All these hopes, however, were frustrated, for
Thugut, now in control of Austrian foreign policy, was intent upon
humiliating and partitioning France and the new conciliatory policy
of Danton was construed by the coalition as a sign of imminent
French collapse. The effort to parley and negotiate with France's
enemies in May and June 1793 was, in truth, a bankrupt one, for
French conquests had by then been lost and French territory invaded.
Danton's diplomacy, at this point, seemed likely to compromise the
whole structure of national defence. When it is remembered that
similar negotiations were undertaken with the leaders of the federalist risings, it is not surprising that the Committee of Public Safety, as
directed by Danton, had become the target of increasing suspicion and
distrust.

(v) *The crisis of national defence and the rise of Hébertism* (*July –August 1793*)

Paradoxically, the new Committee of Public Safety found that,
during July and August, its main anxieties arose in the field of
domestic policy rather than in the conduct of national defence.
This was partly because the Federalist revolts ceased to make
substantial headway, partly because the Austrian and Prussian
commanders failed to make free use of their opportunities, and partly
because the committee itself, under Robespierre's leadership, im-

parted fresh energy to military operations against the rebels and the
the invaders. On the home front, however, the new government had
to withstand the criticism of three vigorous opposition groups—
the *Enragés*, the Dantonists and the Hébertistes. Fresh prominence
was given to the radical movement by the assassination of Marat on
13 July by the Royalist zealot, Charlotte Corday. The *Enragés*
immediately claimed to be Marat's heirs and successors and founded
their own newspapers with the same titles as Marat's journals—
The Publicist and *The People's Friend*. Through these media the
radicals pressed home their demands for the extension of price
controls to the whole range of articles of general consumption and
for more rigorous treatment of counter-revolutionary suspects.
Though the popularity of their leaders was now waning, the *Enragés*
were severe critics of the economic policy of the Committee of Public
Safety and of the lax security measures adopted by the Committee
of General Security. The government, spurred on by these attacks,
found it necessary to make concessions. The first of these was a
decree of 26 July against food hoarders and monopolists. Under this
law the death penalty was prescribed for all who were found guilty
of withholding supplies of specified articles of primary necessity and
municipal anti-hoarding commissions were set up to enforce the
regulations. At the beginning of August the Convention, in order to
evade the demand for the extension of price controls, agreed to
establish in each district barns for storing grain and to allocate
100,000,000 *livres* for grain purchase. In this way the committee
managed to avoid a renewal of sectional disturbances in the capital
without capitulating completely to the economic demands of the
Enragés.

More insidious was the policy of the defeated Dantonists. Danton
himself, although ejected from the Committee of Public Safety, still
remained a powerful political figure and, on the same day that Robespierre entered the committee, 28 July, Danton was elected President
of the Convention. Shortly afterwards, on 1 August, Danton brought
forward a motion that the Committee of Public Safety which he had
created, should be converted into the provisional government of
France and given the free disposal of 100,000,000 *livres*. Although
he himself protested that he had no desire to become a member of
the government once more, Danton may have regarded this strengthening of the executive as desirable if he were re-elected to the
committee. In the meantime if, as he hoped, Robespierre proved
unequal to his new and crushing responsibilities, such a move would

facilitate his overthrow. The motion was, however, rejected. A further effort to embarrass the new committee was made by the Dantonists after the formal promulgation of the new Jacobin constitution on 10 August. On the following day, Delacroix pointed out that the *raison d'être* of the Convention had now disappeared and that, as soon as the electoral register was completed, there was no reason why the Convention should not be dissolved. Robespierre immediately saw the implication and intervened decisively to prolong the powers of the Convention and of the executive. Though the constitution was not officially shelved till 10 October—when the government of France was declared 'revolutionary' for the duration of hostilities— the real threat to the committee was removed at this stage. From these various manœuvres it was clear that Danton and his associates had not accepted their ejection from the Government as an irretrievable defeat and that they regarded themselves in the light of a modern parliamentary opposition.

In August, as the effectiveness of the *Enragés* declined, a new clique of radical politicians led by Hébert took over their social and political programme and made a bid for power. The members of this new connexion were strongly entrenched in the War Department, in the Committee of Public Safety of the department of Paris and in the Commune. They were also successful in dominating the proceedings in the Jacobin club. Hébert himself is chiefly remembered as the editor of the rabid and offensive newspaper, *Le Père Duchesne*. His official post was that of deputy *Procureur-Général* of the Commune, but he had strong ministerial ambitions which had recently been disappointed towards the end of August when Paré, a friend of Danton's, had succeeded Garat as Minister of the Interior. He had a grudge against the Jacobin leaders for the insufficient recognition he had received for the support he had given them in the June crisis. Seizing the opportunity presented by the increasing unpopularity of Varlet and Roux, Hébert set out to capture the political support of the Paris sections by insisting that he would be able to extort from the government the popular demands, which had so far been unsuccessfully championed by the *Enragés*. Greater severity in the treatment of the suspects, the organisation of a Parisian revolutionary army and the application of price control to the goods specified in the anti-hoarding law were articles of the Hébertist programme which had been borrowed from the radicals. To these were added demands for the prosecution of the war *à outrance* and for measures against the financial speculators, who were using their resources to depreciate the *assignats*. As the government's most vulnerable flank Hébert selected for especial attack the Committee of General Security. Alquier, the President, and Basire, the Vice-President, of this committee were suspected, with reason, of being implicated in the royalist intrigues of the baron de Batz, who in the course of August made several attempts to rescue the queen from imprisonment in the Conciergerie prison. Chabot, Julien de Toulouse and Basire were involved in the financial scandals of the East India Company.[1] While these various opposition groups were marshalling their forces for an attack on the government, the new Committee of Public Safety was showing fresh determination and vigour in the conduct of the war. General Gustine was relieved of his command, and eventually executed. On 1 August the garrison of Mayence, which had surrendered with the honours of war a few days earlier, was ordered off to the west of France to fight against the royalist rebels. The systematic devastation of La Vendée was also proclaimed and Pitt denounced by the Convention as 'the enemy of the human race'. Negotiations with the leaders of the federalist risings were broken off and, on 4 August, patriot troops were ordered to march on Lyons. Ten days later, Lazare Carnot—the future 'organiser of victory'—and Prieur de la Côte d'Or were elected to the Committee of Public Safety as military experts. On 23 August the Convention agreed, under pressure from the delegates of the primary assemblies, who had come to Paris for the official celebration of the Jacobin constitution, to order a *levée en masse* of the whole French population. This decree, elaborated by Carnot and Barère, introduced the principle, though not the practice, of the total mobilisation of the country's human and material resources for the purpose of national defence. Although the first article requisitioned the services of the whole civil population, only bachelors and childless widowers between the ages of eighteen and twenty-five were mobilised and organised into battalions on a local basis for the duration of hostilities. It is, therefore, inaccurate to say that the decree established compulsory, universal and permanent military service. The practical genius of Carnot foresaw that the real problem would be, not to raise, but to feed, train and equip the defenders of France, and it is interesting to note that the reservation of key administrative personnel was adopted.

1. A. Soboul, in his monumental work, *Les Sans-Culottes parisiens en L'an II*, Paris, 1958, has, however, shown that 'Hébertism' drew its main strength from spontaneous popular radicalism rather than from Hébert's own political leadership.

(vi) *'Terror the order of the day'* (*September 1793*)

At the end of August and the beginning of September three circumstances combined to present the Hébertists with the opportunity of
enforcing their demands upon the Convention. The general suspicion directed against the Committee of General Security was
confirmed by the apparent reluctance of the government to bring the
Girondin leaders and Marie Antoinette before the Revolutionary
Tribunal. The general arrest of 'suspects' had been decreed by the
Convention, on Danton's motion, on 12 August, but little had been
done by the Committee of General Security to implement the
decision, since the term 'suspect' still lacked legal definition. The
danger of these delays was emphasised by the discovery, on the night
of 2 September, of Rougeville's plot to effect the escape of the queen
from the Conciergerie. Almost simultaneously a fresh bread shortage in the capital was produced by the long summer drought, which
arrested the operation of the flour mills. Here again, however, the
responsible municipal authorities were suspected of corruption in
the management of the food supplies and the case for the
organisation of a 'revolutionary army' was clinched by the difficulty of protecting the food convoys from the outlying districts.
Finally, a further political crisis was precipitated by the receipt of
the news on 2 September of the surrender of Toulon to the English.
The context of revolt thus repeated the now familiar pattern, but the
results were to mark a real watershed in the history of the revolution.

The pressure to which the Convention submitted on 4–6 September was exerted by the Commune of Paris and the Jacobin club,
in both of which organisations Hébertist influence was temporarily
in the ascendant. The petitions from these bodies promoted by
Hébert demanded the incarceration of suspects, the reorganisation
of the Revolutionary Tribunal, the general application of price
controls and the establishment of a 'revolutionary' army. Though
Robespierre, as President of the Convention, attempted to tone down
these demands and to separate the Jacobin club from the malcontents,
Hébertist sympathisers in the Assembly and Danton were able to
command the necessary majorities for the concession of the popular
programme. In some respects, the September crisis merely obliged
the Convention to honour the promises which had been made to the
sans-culottes in June—the trial of the Girondin leaders was agreed to,
the 'revolutionary' army became a reality, and a forced loan of a
milliard *livres* to be levied on the rich was granted. The crisis also
registered the triumph of the Hébertists. The social and economic

policy which they had taken over from the *Enragés* was now implemented, two of their leading representatives in the Convention, Billaud-Varenne and Collot d'Herbois, were elected to the Committee of Public Safety, the Committee of General Security was purged of its suspect members and completely reorganised, and the Revolutionary Tribunal remodelled. On 17 September the long awaited law against the 'suspects'—clarifying their identity and making arrangements for their arrest by the 'revolutionary' committees was passed and, at the end of the month, maximum prices were decreed for the whole range of commodities of general consumption. In a larger sense, the significance of the crisis was that it made possible the Jacobin dictatorship which characterised the subsequent period until the fall of Robespierre. Terror had now been placed 'on the order of the day' and the results were seen in the political trials and executions of the winter months of 1793 and in the passing of the dangers which had threatened the republic's existence since the spring.

I O

THE TERROR, THE FACTIONS AND
THE FALL OF ROBESPIERRE

(i) *The Terror*

In the autumn and winter of 1793 the Terror, to which the Convention had given its official sanction during the September crisis, assumed three forms—a 'political' terror, directed against the agents of federalism and counter-revolution, an 'economic' terror, designed to eliminate currency manipulators and food monopolists, and a 'religious' terror, which the Hébertists turned against organised Christianity. In the capital, the political terror, controlled by the Committee of General Security and by the reorganised Revolutionary Tribunal, was kept within reasonable bounds; in the provinces, where it was in the hands of the representatives *en mission*, the surveillance committees of the communes and the military commissions, it was more vindictive and sporadic. Attempts have been made to assess its 'incidence' on a statistical basis, but detailed regional studies for the whole country have not yet been completed. The excesses committed by Carrier at Nantes, by Fouché at Lyons and by Barras at Toulon should not, therefore, be regarded as characteristic of the period. Many areas of France at this time were comparatively free from excessive violence and the history of these has yet to be written.

The purpose of the 'economic' terror was to ensure that the necessary military supplies should become available at a reasonable cost and also to mitigate, so far as possible, the conflicting interests of urban consumers and agricultural producers. Here again the government tried to steer a middle course between the destruction of suspect financial and commercial undertakings and too rigid a control of food and commodity prices. Some financial concerns associated with the Royalist agent, the baron de Batz, had undoubtedly corrupted the former members of the Committee of General Security and had to be liquidated. Both Prieur de la Côte d'Or and Carnot, however, inside the Committee of Public Safety, were averse to the rigid state control of munition factories and had considerable sympathy with the principles of free commercial enterprise. The 'general maximum' of food and commodity prices, decreed on 29 September, was only accepted by the government under renewed popular pressure and created much administrative friction. With the creation, on 22 October, of a central Food Commission, France was provided with a control agency which proved, in many respects, highly efficient.

By contrast, the attacks on the forms of organised religion in November and December 1793 were promoted by a small group of fanatics led by Chaumette, Fouché and Hébert. The movement was, in fact, a new form of rabble rousing, which played on the anticlericalism of the radical sections in the capital and of the 'revolutionary army'. It had no wide basis of popular support and was effective against the more time-serving officials of the 'constitutional' clergy. The movement began towards the end of September in the department of the Nièvre, where Fouché was acting as *représentant en mission*. The impulse was given by Chaumette, who was then visiting his birthplace, Nevers. After Chaumette had returned to Paris Fouché forbade the performance of any religious ceremonies outside the churches, decreed the destruction of calvaries and crosses, and posted up notices outside the cemeteries that 'death was an eternal sleep'. In November Chaumette committed himself to a campaign for the suppression of Christianity in favour of a new cult of Reason. This secured a limited success when Gobel, the bishop of Paris, was terrorised into resigning office. Shortly afterwards, on 10 November, a so-called festival of Reason was held in the cathedral of Notre Dame.[1] It is clear then that the terror was partly 'official' and partly 'unofficial'. In so far as it was 'unofficial', the government intervened to restrict its scope and to defeat its objectives. Where the government supported the terror, it did so for purely practical reasons. The 'official' political terror, characterised by the great state trials of October and November, sprang from a variety of motives.[2] It was

1. For a brilliant analysis of the real nature and consequences of Dechristianisation, see R. Cobb, *Les Armées Revolutionnaires*, vol. 2, Paris, 1963.
2. The most famous trials were those of the Queen and of the Girondins. Marie

meant to put an end to royalist intrigues and the federalist opposition, to quieten the suspicions of the *sans-culottes* and to convince the Convention that the dictatorship of the Committee of Public Safety was necessary, if anarchy was to be avoided. The control of food and commodity prices, which had been adopted reluctantly, was maintained because it enabled the government to stabilise the paper currency, to effect the purchase of war equipment and supplies economically and to satisfy the claims of the urban proletariat. Similarly, the Convention sanctioned the substitution of a republican for the Gregorian calendar, because it shared the popular prejudices against the 'constitutional' clergy and because it hoped, thereby, to stimulate public interest in the processes of agricultural production. On 6 October, on the motion of Fabre d'Eglantine, the Assembly resolved that the second year of the republic should commence on 22 September 1793, and divided the months into three *décades* of ten days each.[1] On 24 October, further changes were made when the months were renamed after the seasons and the days according to their numerical order in the *décade*. For the names of the saints in the calendar were substituted those of plants, flowers and fruits. These alterations constituted 'one of the most profoundly anti-Christian acts of the revolution'. They were, however, not always as popular as the anti-clericals might have wished. Many of the 'constitutional' clergy refused to transfer the celebration of High Mass from the old to the new sabbath, or *décadi*, and the workers found that the day of rest came once in every ten, instead of every seven, days.

In these respects the terror had secured the support of the government. In others, however, it meant official opposition, which had important effects on the course of political events. The action of the extremist deputies *en mission* in creating unauthorised 'revolutionary' armies, in setting up revolutionary tribunals and their undue reliance on military commissions emphasised the need for greater control from the centre.[2] The result was the attempt to co-ordinate the whole structure of 'revolutionary' government, by subordinating

Antionette was guillotined on 16 October and the Girondins on the 31st. These were followed in November by Bailly, Barnave and a series of unsuccessful revolutionary generals.

1. This left five days at the end of the year, renamed *sans-culottides*.
2. The 'revolutionary' tribunals dealt with crimes of counter-revolution. Their characteristic was that they dispensed with the use of a 'grand jury' or *jury d'accusation*. The military commissions dealt with rebels captured under arms, under the decree of 19 March 1793.

its agents to the Committee of Public Safety. By a decree of 4 December 1793, this committee was given the control of ministers, the right, subject to the approval of the Convention, to nominate generals, to direct foreign policy and to purge the local authorities. The machinery of local government was simplified by confining the departments to purely routine administration and by making the districts responsible for the execution of 'revolutionary' decrees. The proctors (*procureux*) of the districts and communes were replaced by 'national agents' who were the representatives of the central power. This was a shrewd blow against the independent authority of the powerful Paris Commune. The provision that, in Paris, the 'revolutionary' committees' should correspond directly with and be subject to the control of the Committee of General Security weakened the Commune's relations with the sections. The Commune was also deprived of the power of dispatching commissioners to the provinces. The representatives *en mission* were forbidden to delegate their powers, to create 'revolutionary' armies, or to fix local prices. Supplementary circulars reminded them that they must submit to the resolutions of the Committee of Public Safety and that their previously unlimited powers had now been restricted. Special arrangements were made for the prompt dispatch of decrees to the local authorities and for regular ten-day reports from the latter to the executive committees of the Convention. On paper, the rigid administrative centralisation, which had collapsed in the summer of 1789, was once more restored. It remained to be seen, however, whether the Committee of General Security at the centre, or the representatives *en mission* in the provinces would accept this new subordination. It was, in fact, the revolt of these authorities which contributed powerfully to the fall of Robespierre in July 1794.

Meanwhile, the progress of the movement for dechristianisation had caused the government much anxiety. The Committee of Public Safety was well aware that the majority of Frenchmen still remained loyal to the forms of Roman Catholicism, and it was easy to anticipate that the 'religious' terror would be a source of social confusion and political division. Robespierre himself led the attack on Chaumette and Fouché, decrying them as atheists and pointing out that their activities would encourage counter-revolution in France and deepen the hostility to the revolution abroad. The government was prepared to strip the church towers of their bells in order to cast cannon and to despoil the churches of their silver and jewels for the sake of the national treasury. It was prepared to acquiesce in the voluntary abdication of the constitutional clergy, but it drew the line at the use of violence against the priests. When bad news came through from La Vendée at the end of November, the Convention even accepted the decision of the Commune to close the churches in Paris. By that time, however, Robespierre had decided, at all costs, to terminate the religious terror, and in this he was supported, for ulterior motives, by Danton.

(ii) *The Dantonists and the policy of 'clemency'*

Fortunately for Robespierre, the Hébertist group of anti-religious fanatics was suspected of complicity in a so-called 'foreign plot', which had been denounced by Fabre d'Eglantine, a friend of Danton, on 12 October. Among those who had forced Gobel to resign his functions as bishop of Paris, Anacharsis Cloots was a Prussian and Pereira a Portuguese Jew. Other associates were also of foreign origin and it was, therefore, easy for Robespierre to accuse them of being in league with France's enemies. The fact that the followers of Danton had connived at the falsification of a decree of the Convention concerned with the liquidation of the East India Company, also recoiled upon the heads of the Hébertist faction. After Chabot and Basire had denounced their colleague, Delaunay, to the Committee of General Security, all three were arrested on suspicion on 17 November.[1] This news brought Danton back to Paris from his home at Arcis. Seeing Robespierre in full cry against the Hébertists, Danton joined in the attack in order to divert attention from his own corrupt friends and associates. This temporary alliance with Robespierre, however, was also intended by Danton to alienate the great 'incorruptible' from his Hébertist colleagues in the Committee of Public Safety—Collot d'Herbois and Billaud-Varenne. Once the committee had been split over the issue of dechristianisation, the way would have been open for Danton to re-enter the government and to put an end to the 'political' terror. This was now his chief objective, for he wished, not only to save his friends from the fate that threatened them, but also to substitute for the policy of terror one of 'clemency' and conciliation.

To save Chabot, Basire and Delaunay, Danton determined to exploit the general feeling which had by then developed against the wholesale arrests of suspects carried out since September. He did so through the columns of Camille Desmoulins' famous news-sheet or

1. The real author of the falsification of the decree was Fabre d'Eglantine, whose guilt was only discovered in January 1794.

broadside—*Le Vieux Cordelier*, the first number of which appeared on 5 December 1793. In this Desmoulins attacked the Hébertists, not only as the agents of the religious terror, but also as the fomenters of treason. The policy of 'clemency' was brilliantly outlined in the third issue of the news-sheet of 15 December. Desmoulins' invective was directed particularly against the law of suspects, which had been passed under pressure from the Hébertists and against the law of 4 December, which had been passed on the motion of Billaud-Varenne. Quick success attended the combined efforts of the Dantonists. On 17 December several prominent Hébertists, including Vincent, Ronsin, the commander of the Parisian 'revolutionary' army, and Maillard were arrested. On 20 December the Convention was induced to establish a 'committee of clemency'. This was instructed to scrutinise the lists of those who had been recently arrested in order that those found innocent could be released. Its members were to be nominated by the Committees of Public Safety and General Security.[1] A week later, Gaudon, a wine merchant, who was liable to the death penalty for offences against the anti-hoarding law, was acquitted and the law itself was re-drafted so as to make the penalties less severe. In these developments Robespierre seems to have acquiesced largely because his hatred of dechristianisation blinded him temporarily to the political manœuvres of the Dantonists.

The Hébertists, however, marshalled their forces for a counter-attack. On 21 December Collot d'Herbois made a hurried return to the capital from Lyons, where he had been giving a hand with the firing-squads, and made a spirited attack on the Dantonists at the Jacobin club, being seconded by Hébert. This had the effect of arousing Robespierre's suspicions of the trap laid for him by the 'Indulgents' and, on 26 December, Collot and Billaud-Varenne persuaded the Convention to abolish the 'committee of clemency'. Further reverses for the Dantonists followed. Camille Desmoulins, in defending the policy of his news-sheet at the Jacobin club, violently quarrelled with his old school-fellow, Robespierre; Fabre d'Eglantine was implicated in the financial scandals and arrested on the night of 12 January 1794, while the Committee of General Security revived and pressed the charges against Chabot, Basire and Delaunay. On 2 February Vincent and Ronsin were set at liberty. The Dantonist manœuvres had by then been fully exposed, but the final discredit

1. Robespierre approved the suggestion with two reservations—namely, that only true patriots' should be released, and that the committee should be secret.

and overthrow of the faction was made inevitable by the irrespons-
ible attacks of Desmoulins on the Committee of Public Safety, the
'republican Jansenism' of Robespierre and the whole system of
'revolutionary' government.[1]

(iii) *The fall of the factions*

The political importance of the dechristianisation movement was that
it had facilitated the skilful opposition tactics of Danton and Desmoulins. These had failed, but there can be no doubt that they had
seriously compromised the whole position of the executive government. The Dantonists had thrown their weight with the committees against the Hébertists, in order not merely to check the extremists
but also to weaken the government by robbing it of the support of the
sans-culottes. They had successfully played upon the divergent
political connexions of the members of the Committee of Public
Safety, and had made the conduct of Robespierre appear vacillating
and lacking in consistency. They had advocated a policy of reaching
a peaceful settlement with France's enemies, which had evoked
considerable popular sympathy at a time when French victories
seemed to make negotiations at last possible. They had pleaded for
clemency and an end of the terror at a period when the federalist
revolt was collapsing and Toulon had been recaptured by Bonaparte
from the English. Their policy, which had appeared unstatesmanlike
in the summer of 1793, seemed to offer a real and practical alternative
to continued war, of which the objectives had become less clear.

Until recently historians attributed to Robespierre the political
tactics which had, in fact, been employed by Danton. The former
was supposed to have sided with Danton in order to discredit the
Hébertists and then to have turned on the 'Indulgents'. Once he
had penetrated the political designs of Danton, however, Robespierre
delivered a simultaneous frontal attack on both the rival factions
in great speeches made on 25 December 1793 and 5 February 1794.
These marked his return to the policy of a *via media*, which the Committee of Public Safety had endeavoured to follow ever since the
overthrow of the Girondins. In the spring of 1794 Robespierre and
the government found it necessary to liquidate the Hébertists before
they dealt with the 'Indulgents', but that was because they presented
the more immediate danger. The Hébertists took the initiative in

1. The government of France had been 'revolutionary', i.e. provisional, since the
suspension of the Jacobin constitution of 1793. On 10 October 1793, the Convention
had decreed that this system should operate for the duration of hostilities with Europe.

March more in a spirit of desperation than from a consciousness of their own strength. Since Chaumette had become *agent national* for Paris, he had felt it wise to hold aloof from his former associates. The movement for dechristianisation had lost a good deal of its impulse and the Hébertists had been discredited by their alleged connexion with the 'foreign plot'. When, at the beginning of March, Ronsin, Vincent and Hébert began to plan an insurrection on the model of 31 May 1793, they had to rely for pretexts on an artificially stimulated shortage of vegetables and meat in Paris and on an attempt to rouse the prison population. They had little support in the sections, none at all from the Commune, and Collot d'Herbois and Billaud-Varenne in the Government abandoned them at the crucial moment. As signs of an impending *journée* accumulated, the Government, for the first time in the history of the revolution, took effective preventive action by nipping the conspiracy in the bud. On 14 March Hébert and his followers were arrested and sent before the Revolutionary Tribunal. After a summary trial Hébert, Vincent, Ronsin, Momoro and fourteen of their collaborators were guillotined on 25 March and Chaumette on 13 April. The Hébertists fell amid popular indifference, partly because the campaigns of Desmoulins had had their effect, and partly because the Jacobin club dissociated itself from a movement organised in the Cordelier club. Nevertheless, the action of the government in disbanding the 'revolutionary' army and in purging the Commune of Hébertist influence, left the *sans-culottes* with a feeling of sullen dissatisfaction.[1]

Meanwhile, the Committee of General Security had reported on the Dantonist clique involved in the financial scandals, and on 19 March the Convention had indicted Fabre d'Eglantine, Delaunay, Basire, Chabot and Julien of Toulouse. Though Robespierre's affection for Desmoulins made him hesitate to seal the fate of the 'Indulgents', Billaud-Varenne and Collot d'Herbois had no such compunctions. The case against the moderate faction was laid before the two great committees on 30 March by Saint-Just, and the Convention thereupon ordered the arrest of Danton, Delacroix, Desmoulins and Philippeaux as accomplices of Fabre and Chabot. Another charge preferred against the Dantonists was that of complicity in the 'foreign plot'. The trial lasted from 2 to 5 April and had to be hurriedly terminated as Danton's eloquence made a deep impression on the jury. In the last analysis, the accused were condemned on

1. For a detailed analysis of the significance of the Hébertist trials, see A. Soboul, *Les Sans-Culottes parisiens en l'an II*, pp. 762–872.

political grounds and were guillotined on 5 April. Having decided on
the elimination of the Hébertists, the government could not have
allowed the Dantonists to survive, for their acquittal would have
meant its downfall. The weight which was placed on the destruction
of both factions was indicated by a decree of 1 April, putting an
end to the executive council of ministers and substituting for it
twelve executive commissions rigidly controlled by the Committee
of Public Safety. This constitutional reorganisation was a political
blow directed against Hébertist influence in the War Department and
Dantonist influence in the ministries of the Interior and of Foreign
Affairs.

(iv) The ascendancy and fall of Robespierre (13 April–27 July 1794)

The period between the final extermination of the Dantonist faction
of 13 April and the overthrow of Robespierre on 27 July was dominated by three political factors of primary importance. These were
the deep rift which appeared among the members of the Committee of
Public Safety, the increasing friction between this committee and the
Committee of General Security and Robespierre's failure to command the continued support of the 'Plain' or moderate section in the
Convention. It is largely in terms of these developments that the
crisis of 9 Thermidor may be best understood.

For the time being, the elimination of the rival factions left the
Committee of Public Safety, and particularly Robespierre, in a position of unchallengeable authority. Much depended, however, on
the committee's ability to restrain the multiplying differences of its
members on matters of general policy, and on Robespierre's use of
his personal ascendancy in the government. A split in the committee
had already developed over social and economic policy. At the end of
February and the beginning of March Saint-Just, Couthon and Robespierre had identified themselves with a project for the free distribution
to impoverished patriots of the landed property of proved 'suspects'.
It seems probable that this scheme, together with a new law for the
control of general commodity prices and further legislation against
the monopolists, formed part of a programme of social reforms
designed to rob the Hébertists of the support of the sans-culottes. If
such was the intention, the policy failed, since the Hébertists had
to be dealt with by force and the sans-culottes remained impassive.
Nevertheless, on 26 February, the Convention decided, on Saint-
Just's motion, that the 'suspects' should be imprisoned till the peace
and then banished, and that, meanwhile, their estates should be

confiscated. On 3 March the Assembly provided that popular commissions should be set up to inquire into the guilt of those accused of counter-revolutionary activities. The free distribution of the confiscated estates was not approved and, in fact, these 'laws of Ventôse' were never implemented. The operation would have affected about 300,000 'suspects', not all of whom possessed landed property, and both Carnot and Prieur de la Côte d'Or, inside the committee, were strenuously opposed to such a large-scale measure of public relief. The discussions did much to consolidate the close working alliance in the committee of Couthon, Saint-Just and Robespierre and to oppose them to the rest of their colleagues.

This division was accentuated and the personal isolation of Robespierre emphasised when the latter induced the Convention, on 7 May, to organise a series of public festivals to celebrate the inauguration of a new civic religion. The existence of a deity was proclaimed and the immortality of the soul recognised. The initiative had been taken partly to repudiate the atheism professed by the Hébertists and partly to give practical force to the religious conceptions of Rousseau. Robespierre's opponents, however, interpreted his move as a cautious attempt to reintroduce the forms and beliefs of Roman Catholicism.[1] To others, it seemed to involve a rejection of the principle of liberty of worship, and there were many who suspected that dissentients from this personal dogma of Robespierre would be subjected to persecution. These suspicions seemed to be confirmed, when the first of the public festivals—that of the Supreme Being—was held on 8 June, the Feast of the Holy Sacrament. A vast procession, organised by the painter, David, was headed by Robespierre as temporary president of the Convention, on its way from the Tuileries to the Champ de Mars. The airs and graces which Robespierre displayed on this occasion alienated many members of the Convention and contributed greatly to the feeling of his colleagues that he now regarded himself both as a pontiff and as a dictator.

The next measure sponsored by Robespierre and Couthon may be said finally to have alienated the other members of the Committee of Public Safety. This was the famous decree of 22 Prairial, expediting the procedure of the Revolutionary Tribunal in Paris, passed on 10 June 1794. Some historians believe that the procedure of the Revolutionary Tribunal was abbreviated because the pre-

---

1. M. A. Mathiez, who spent a lifetime defending Robespierre's reputation, regarded this step as 'a happy attempt to reconcile believers with the republic'. *Robespierre Terroriste*, p. 33.

liminary stages in the trial of 'enemies of the people' had already been delegated to the popular commissions established under the laws of *ventôse*. Others suggest that Robespierre wished to repudiate the policy of 'clemency', which his contemporaries had said would follow the inauguration of the civic religion. Another explanation is that the law was an act of reprisal for attempts made on Robespierre's life towards the end of May.[1] The decree relieved the Revolutionary Tribunal of the obligation of interrogating accused persons before public trial and made the hearing of witnesses optional: it deprived the accused of defence counsel and provided that the sole punishment for those found guilty would be death.[2] Nothing was said about the securities which had hitherto ensured that members of the Convention could not be brought before the tribunal without a special decree of accusation passed by the legislature.[3] Other provisions greatly extended the scope of the prosecution by the vagueness of the crimes which were now treated as counter-revolutionary. Couthon had drafted the law and Robespierre had prevented its adjournment only by leaving his presidential chair in the Convention to intervene in the debate. The other members of the committee subsequently stated that they had not been consulted.[4] The weight of the evidence is against this defence, but it is significant that, immediately the law had passed, Robespierre absented himself for a month from meetings of the Convention and shortly afterwards ceased to attend the Committee of Public Safety. By that time both Saint-Just and Robespierre had quarrelled violently with Carnot over the conduct of military operations and it had become difficult to conceal these dissensions from the general public.

Equally serious was the growing friction between the two great executive committees. Although these worked in close association, and often held joint sessions for the discussion of high policy, all attempts clearly to delimit their respective spheres of action had failed. Since July 1793 the Committee of Public Safety had exercised the right of summoning and arresting persons, which the Convention had originally vested in the Committee of General Security. When, in

1. An individual named Admiral had made one attempt on 20 May, and, three days later, a woman, Cécile Renault, had been arrested on a similar charge.

2. Couthon defended the suppression of defence counsel by arguing that they had charged their clients inordinate fees and that they had turned the Revolutionary Tribunal into a sounding-board for anti-revolutionary demonstrations.

3. Article 10 of the decree was ambiguous, and historians are still divided on the question whether the law did infringe the principle of parliamentary immunity.

4. But both Barère and Billaud-Varenne supported the law when it was discussed in the Convention.

September 1793, the police committee had been purged of its corrupt members, its personnel had been nominated by the Committee of Public Safety, and not elected, as hitherto, by the Convention. In the spring of 1794 this ascendancy of the Committee of Public Safety, reaffirmed in the law of 4 December 1793, had steadily increased. It is significant, for example, that, whereas the great state trials of the autumn of 1793 had been prepared by the police committee, the case against the Dantonists had been entrusted to Saint-Just. The law of 22 Prairial had not even mentioned the Committee of General Security, and when Saint-Just, Couthon and Robespierre established a special police section of the Committee of Public Safety towards the end of April, the strain between the two committees reached breaking point. Although the complete centralisation of authority in the Committee of Public Safety was in the spirit of 'revolutionary' government, and in the logic of events, the organisation which the older police committee had built up was too elaborate and strongly entrenched for its power to be eliminated—especially when the Committee of Public Safety lacked coherence and unity. The result was a combination of Robespierre's enemies in both committees to overthrow the triumvirate.

In the final analysis, however, the fall of Robespierre and his associates must be attributed to their loss of control over the Convention. Many members of the legislative assembly had never forgiven the Jacobins for the expulsion of the Girondins, others had been gravely disturbed by the destruction of the Dantonists, and the majority had been disconcerted by the mass trials and executions, which had followed the promulgation of the law of 22 Prairial.[1] Robespierre had been mainly responsible for the recall of several of the most powerful representatives on mission—Carrier from Nantes, Tallien from Bordeaux, Barras and Fréron from Toulon, Fouché from Lyons, Lebon from Arras, and Rovère from the department of the Vaucluse. Some of these had been expelled from the Jacobin club and most of them feared the fate of the Dantonists. Meanwhile, General Jourdan's decisive victory over the Austrians at the battle of Fleurus on 26 June had ensured the reconquest of Belgium, which quickly followed. These victories convinced the moderate members

---

1. The final or 'great' Terror was initiated by the trial and execution of those concerned in the conspiracy of the royalist agent, the baron de Batz, in the middle of June. In June and July 1794 the guillotine claimed 1,285 victims and only 20 per cent of those brought before the Revolutionary Tribunal were acquitted. These figures are explained by a recrudescence of alleged prison conspiracies, by the effort to liquidate the aristocracy and by the attempts on Robespierre's life.

of the Convention that the terror had outlived its usefulness. The tyranny of the Committee of Public Safety and the 'dictatorship' of Robespierre thus became intolerable. The final plans for the overthrow of the Robespierrists were laid, on the night of 26 July, by the members of the two great committees, after Robespierre had antagonised the Convention during the day by vague threats and accusations against his enemies. The conspirators decided to deprive Hanriot of his command of the Parisian National Guard, to arrest both him and Dumas, president of the Revolutionary Tribunal, and, above all, to prevent Robespierre and Saint-Just from defending themselves in the Assembly. Members of the 'Plain' and the Right agreed to co-operate and the fall of Robespierre and his associates thus took on the character, less of a *coup d'état*, than of the overthrow of a ministry.[1] These arrangements were successfully carried through on 9 Thermidor (27 July), largely because the Commune proved incapable of resisting the Convention, and because Hanriot lost his nerve. On the evening of 28 July Robespierre, Saint-Just and Couthon were executed and their fate was shared, in the days which followed, by eighty-seven members of the Commune.

(v) *Conclusion*

The revolution can hardly be said to have run its course until Bonaparte seized power from the successors of the Thermidorians in November 1799. Limits of space, however, preclude any attempt here even to summarise the history of the intervening years, in which the revolution lost its impetus and changed its character. Until the establishment of the executive Directory on 28 October 1795, France continued to be ruled under the forms of 'revolutionary government'. Although the word 'terror' was expunged from its official documents after Thermidor, and the law of Prairial abolished, the Convention still governed by means of repression and the horrors of the 'red' Terror were recalled by the 'white' Terror of reaction. Significant political and social changes, however, followed the fall of Robespierre. The surviving Girondins were recalled to the Convention and their influence was felt in the restoration of the departmental authorities to their former independence in local government

---

1. Robespierre himself was partly to blame for this outcome, for he had insisted on submitting the differences between his group and the rest of the committees to the Convention, apparently relying on the support of the right, whose members he had assiduously protected. It was this obstinacy which wrecked the last-minute attempts, made on 22 and 23 July, to reconcile the differences between the triumvirate and the rest of the Committee of Public Safety.

and in the destruction of the autonomy of the Parisian commune.[1] In September 1794 state support was withdrawn from the 'constitutional' clergy, and the virtual separation of Church and State proclaimed. The Committee of General Security recovered from the Committee of Public Safety its former independent control over the political police, the committees of the convention were remodelled and each was given control over one of the executive commissions. The Jacobin club was closed and the 'revolutionary' committees reorganised. In May 1795 the Revolutionary Tribunal was abolished, in order to facilitate the negotiations for a general peace. The 'economic' terror was also relaxed and the attempt to control general prices abandoned. Meanwhile, the *émigrés* had begun to find their way back to France, with official connivance—but only to carry on the struggle against the democratic republicans. In a larger sense, Thermidor marked the recapture of political control by the middle-class 'notables'. The Constitution of 1795 was largely their work, and it was with their blessing that Bonaparte re-endowed France with the forms of autocracy. Under the Directory, France struggled to avoid dictatorship, but a régime of repeated *coups d'état* made dictatorship appear preferable to either Jacobinism or royalist reaction, especially when the social and economic conquests of the revolution were thereby preserved for those who had been its main beneficiaries—the middle classes.

In our own time the French revolution of 1789 has been overshadowed by the Russian revolution of 1917 and its ideals were temporarily dimmed or distorted by the Fascist and Nazi revolutions. Critics inside France have spurned its emphasis upon the primacy of the individual in relation to society and the state, while foreign observers have asked whether it was, after all, 'a mistake' and whether the price which France had to pay for its conquest of liberty and equality was too great. Historians are more disposed to bring the revolution of 1789 into focus by comparative studies of other eighteenth-century revolutions, of which there were many, and by emphasising that its essential contribution to the evolution of modern democracy was that it enunciated the principle and worked out the implications of popular sovereignty. Only in a limited sense can the French revolution be regarded as the source of modern totalitarianism, for the Jacobin dictatorship and the 'revolutionary government' of 1793 were merely the provisional and abnormal

1. It was not until the revolution of 1830 that Paris recovered its political supremacy in the life of the French nation.

forms to which France submitted, in time of civil and foreign war, for the defence of its national security and its essentially liberal ideas. In submitting to the rule of the minority, and in accepting terror as a means of government, France did not deny the principles of 1789, for those principles had never been regarded as abstract and immutable, apart from circumstances. The liberal experiment of 1789 failed because Louis XVI refused to accept the role of constitutional monarch and because the aristocracy refused to bow before the consequences of political equality. In a very real sense, the revolution had been from the beginning and remained to the end 'a merciless conflict between aristocracy and democracy'.[1]

---

1. For surveys of recent interpretations of the revolution see M. Reinhard, 'Sur l'histoire de la Révolution française, Travaux récents et perspectives', *Annales*, vol. XIV (1959), pp. 553–90, and G. Rudé, *Interpretations of the French Revolution*, 1961 (Historical Association pamphlet G.47). For the historiography of revolutionary studies see ch. XXII of vol. VIII of the *New Cambridge Modern History* by J. McManners.

SELECT BIBLIOGRAPHY

The available literature on the French Revolution is immense. The best short guide to recent works of specialised scholarship is J. Godechot, *Les Revolutions 1770–1799*, (Paris, 1963), (Collection 'Nouvelle Clio', No. 36). See also *A Select List of Works on Europe and Europe Overseas, 1715–1815*, ed. J. S. Bromley and A. Goodwin (Oxford, 1956). The outstanding work on the subject is the late Professor G. Lefebvre's *La Révolution Française* (vol. XIII in *Peuples et Civilisations*, ed. L. Halpen and P. Sagnac, 3rd edition revised 1963). It is now available in English translation as *The French Revolution: From its origins to 1793* (trans. E. M. Evanson) and *The French Revolution: from 1793 to 1799* (trans. J. H. Stewart and J. Friguglietti), (London and New York, 1962 and 1964). J. M. Thompson's *The French Revolution* (Oxford 1943), which for long ranked as the best single volume treatment in English, has been overtaken by more recent research.

I: INTRODUCTORY

SALVEMINI, G., *The French Revolution, 1788–1792*, trans. from Italian by I. M. Rawson (London, 1954)

HOBSBAWM, E. J., *The Age of Revolution. Europe from 1789 to 1848* (London, 1962)

RUDE, G., *Revolutionary Europe, 1783–1815* (London, 1964)

SYDENHAM, M. J., *The French Revolution* (London, 1965)

II: GENERAL WORKS

ACTON, LORD, *Lectures on the French Revolution* (Cambridge, 1910)

AULARD, F. A., *Political History of the French Revolution*, trans. B. Miall, 4 vols. (London, 1910)

MATHIEZ, A., *The French Revolution*, trans. C. A. Phillips (New York, 1928)

SAGNAC, P., *La Révolution française, 1789–1792*, vol. I of *Histoire de France contemporaine*, ed. E. Lavisse (Paris, 1920)

PARISET, G., *La Révolution française, 1792–1799*, vol. II in same series (Paris, 1920)

SOREL, A., *L'Europe et la révolution française*, 8 vols. (1885–1904, 23rd edition 1942). A classic work, though superseded for the period 1795–9 by modern scholarship.

JAURES, J., *Histoire Socialiste de la révolution française*, ed. A. Mathiez, 8 vols. (1922–4). The fountain-head of the modern study of the social history of the revolution and the inspiration behind Lefebvre's researches

MOUSNIER, R. and LABROUSSE, C. E., *Le XVIIIe Siècle*, vol. 5 in M. Crouzet's *Histoire Générale des Civilisations* (Paris, 1953)

GOODWIN, A., ed. *The American and French Revolutions, 1763–1793 (New Cambridge Modern History*, vol. VIII (Cambridge, 1965)

LEFEBVRE, G., *Études sur la Révolution française* (1954). A valuable collection of his most important articles on various aspects of the period

GODECHOT, J., *La Grande Nation. L'expansion révolutionnaire de la France dans le monde, 1789–1799*, 2 vols. (1956)

GÖHRING, M., *Die Grosse Revolution*, 2 vols. (Tübingen, 1948–50). First-rate treatment of the Ancien Régime

The most recent general surveys include A. Soboul's Marxist study *La Révolution française*, vol. I: *De la Bastille à la Gironde*; vol. II: *De la Montagne à Brumaire* (1964) and A. Cobban's, *The Social Interpretation of the French Revolution* (Cambridge, 1964), which is a controversial but stimulating onslaught on the Marxist historians of the revolution. N. Hampson's *A Social History of the French Revolution* (Manchester, 1963) is an authoritative and judicious study

III: BIOGRAPHICAL STUDIES
(All in French, unless place of publication indicates otherwise)

Barère, L. Gershoy, Princeton (New Jersey, 1962)

Barnave, Miss E. D. Bradby, 2 vols. (Oxford, 1915; J. J. Chevallier (1936)

Brissot, Miss E. Ellery (Cambridge, Mass., 1915)

Calonne, P. Jolly (1949); R. Lacour-Gayet (1963)

Carnot, M. Reinhard, 2 vols. (1950–2)

Condorcet, L. Cahen (1904); J. S. Schapiro, (New York, 1934); J. Bouissounouse (1962)

Danton, L. Madelin (1914); L. Barthou (1932)

Dumouriez, A. Chuquet (1914)

Fouché, L. Madelin, 2 vols. (1900)

Hébert, G. Walter (1946); L. Jacob (1960)

Lafayette, E. Charavay (1898); L. Gottschalk, 4 vols. (Chicago, 1935–51)

Marat, L. Gottschalk (New York, 1927); G. Walter (1933); J. Massin (1960)

Marie Antionette, C. Kunstler (1938); Arnaud-Boutteloup (1924)

Mirabeau, A. Stern, 2 vols. (1895); J. J. Chevallier (1947); B. Erdmannsdörfer, Leipzig (1950); O. J. G. Welch (London, 1951)

Necker, E. Lavaquery (1933); E. Chapuisat (1938); P. Jolly (1947)

Robespierre, J. M. Thompson (Oxford, 1939); J. Massin (1956); M. Bouloiseau (1956); G. Walter, 2 vols. (1961)

Sieyès, J. H. Clapham (London, 1912); P. Bastid (1939)

Saint-Just, E. M. Curtis (New York, 1925); G. Bruun (New York, 1932); A. Ollivier (1954)

Talleyrand, Duff-Cooper (London, 1937); G. Lacour-Gayet, 3 vols. (1947)

Vergniaud, E. Lintilhac (1920)

IV: SPECIAL STUDIES
Chapters 1–3

ALEXIS DE TOCQUEVILLE, *L'Ancien Régime et la Révolution (Oeuvres Complètes*, ed. J. P. Mayer, with introduction by G. Lefebvre) (1952)

METHIVIER, H., *L'Ancien Régime* (Paris, 1961). (Series *Que Sais-je?* no. 925—a helpful and succinct analysis of recent work on the subject)

SAGNAC, P., *La formation de la société française moderne*, vol. 2, 1715–1789 (1946)

BARBER, E. G., *The Bourgeoisie in XVIII century France* (Princeton, 1955)

FORSTER, R., *The Nobility of Toulouse in the Eighteenth Century* (Baltimore, 1960)

MARION, M., *Histoire financière de la France, 1715–85*, vol. I (1914)

LABROUSSE, C. E., *Esquisse des mouvements des prix et revenus en France au XVIII siècle*, 2 vols. (1933)
—— *La crise de l'économie française à la fin de l'Ancien Régime et au début de la Révolution* (1944)
DAKIN, D., *Turgot and the Ancien Régime in France* (London, 1939)
BOSHER, J. F., *The Single Duty Project. A Study of the Movement for a French Customs Union in the Eighteenth Century* (London, 1964)
MATTHEWS, G. T., *The Royal General Farms in Eighteenth-century France* (Columbia, 1958)
MCCLOY, S. T., *Government Assistance in Eighteenth-century France* (Durham, N.C., 1946)
—— *The Humanitarian Movement in Eighteenth-century France* (Lexington, 1957)
BLOCH, M., *Les caractères originaux de l'histoire rurale française*, 2 vols. (1953–6)
YOUNG, A., *Travels in France and Italy, 1787–90*, ed. C. Maxwell (Cambridge, 1929)
MORNET, D., *Les origines intellectuelles de la révolution française* (1932)
COBBAN, A., *In Search of Humanity. The role of the Enlightenment in Modern History* (London, 1960)
GAY, P., *Voltaire's Politics. The Poet as Realist* (Princeton, 1959)
—— *The Party of Humanity, Studies in the French Enlightenment* (London, 1964)
WILSON, A. M., *Diderot. The Testing Years, 1713–1759* (Oxford, 1957)
GREEN, F. C., *J. J. Rousseau* (Cambridge, 1955)
MAUZI, R., *L'idée de bonheur dans la littérature et la pensée française au XVIII siècle* (1960)
MOUSNIER, R., *Progrès Scientifique et technique au XVIIIᵉ siècle* (1958)
BLUCHE, F., *Les magistrats du Parlement de Paris au XVIIIᵉ siècle* (Besançon, 1960)
PALMER, R. R., *Catholics and Unbelievers in XVIII century France* (Princeton, 1939)
—— *The Age of the Democratic Revolution. A political history of Europe and America, 1760–1800*, vol. 1. (Princeton, 1959)
LOUGH, J., *An Introduction to Eighteenth-century France* (London, 1960)
MCMANNERS, J., *French Ecclesiastical Society under the Ancien Régime* (Manchester, 1960)
CARCASSONE, E., *Montesquieu et le problème de la constitution française au XVII siècle* (1927)
LÉONARD, E. G., *L'armée et ses problèmes au XVIII siècle* (1958)
RENOUVIN, P., *Les assemblées provinciales de 1787* (1921)
CHÉREST, A., *La chute de l'ancien régime*, 3 vols. (1884)
GLAGAU, H., *Reformversuche und Sturz des Absolutismus in Frankreich, 1774–88* (Munich, 1908)
LEFEBVRE, G., *The Coming of the French Revolution*, trans. R. R. Palmer (Princeton, 1949)
BECKER, O., *Die Verfassungspolitik der französischen Regierung der grossen Revolution* (Berlin, 1910)
COBBAN, A., *Ambassadors and Secret Agents* (London, 1954)
EGRET, J., *La Pré-Révolution Française, 1787–1788* (1962)

Chapters 4–5
BRAESCH, F., *1789, L'année cruciale* (1940)
LEFEBVRE, G., *Les paysans du Nord pendant la révolution française*, 2 vols. (1924, re-printed in 1 vol, 1959)
—— *La Grande Peur* (1932)
—— *Etudes Orléanaises*, vol I—*Contribution à l'étude des structures sociales à la fin du XVIII siècle* (1962), vol. II, *Subsistances et Maximum; 1789—An. IV* (1963)
DE SAINT JACOB, P., *Les paysans de la Bourgogne du Nord au XVIII siècle* (1961)
BOIS, P., *Les paysans de l'Ouest* (1960)
DARD, E., *La chute de la royauté* (1950)
EGRET, J., *La révolution des Notables. Mounier et les Monarchiens* (1950)

DUMONT, E., *Souvenirs sur Mirabeau et sur les deux premières assemblées législatives* ed. J. Bénétruy (1950)
—— *L'Atelier de Mirabeau. Quatre proscrits Genevois dans la tourmente revolution-naire* (Geneva, 1962)
SAGNAC, P., *La législation civile de la révolution française* (1898)
RUDE, G., *The Crowd in the French Revolution* (Oxford, 1959)
POLAND, B. C., *French Protestantism and the French Revolution* (Princeton, 1957)
GODECHOT, J., *La Contre-Révolution, 1789–1804* (1961)

Chapters 6–7
GODECHOT, J., *Les institutions de la France sous la Révolution et l'Empire* (1951)
DESLANDRES, M., *Histoire constitutionelle de la France de 1789 à 1870*, vol. I (1932)
GOOCH, R. K., *Parliamentary Government in France, 1789–1791* (Ithaca, New York, 1960)
GARAUD, M., *Histoire général du droit privé français*, vol. I (1953,) vol. 2 (1959)
LATREILLE, A., *L'Eglise catholique et la Révolution française*, vol. I (1946)
MATHIEZ, A., *Rome et le clergé français sous la Constituante* (1911)
ERDMANN, K. D., *Volkssouveränität und Kirche* (Cologne, 1949)
LEFLON, J., *La crise révolutionnaire, 1789–1846* vol. XX, *Histoire de l'Eglise*, ed. Fliche (1949)
AIMOND, C., *L'énigme de Varennes* (1950)
MATHIEZ, A., *Le club des Cordeliers pendant la crise de Varennes* (1913)
RAIN, P., *La diplomatic française de Mirabeau à Bonaparte* (1950)
CLAPHAM, J. H., *The causes of the war of 1792* (Cambridge, 1899)
GLAGAU, H., *Die Französische Legislative und der Ursprung der Revolutionskriege* (Berlin, 1896)
HARRIS, S. E., *The Assignats* (Cambridge, Mass., 1930)
SAGNAC, P., *La chute de la royauté* (1909)
MATHIEZ, A., *Girondins et Montagnards* (1930)
SYDENHAM, M. J., *The Girondins* (London, 1961)
FUGIER, A., *La Révolution française et l'Empire Napoléonien* (vol. IV of *Histoire des Relations Internationales*, ed. P. Renouvin) (1954)
SOBOUL, A., *Les soldats de l'an II* (1960)

Chapters 8–9
MATHIEZ, A., *Le Dix Août* (1911)
BRAESCH, F., *La commune du dix Août* (1911)
CARON, P., *Les massacres de Septembre* (1935)
SELIGMAN, E., *La justice en France pendant la révolution*, 2 vols. (1913)
TILLY, C., *The Vendée* (London, 1964)
GREER, D., *The incidence of the Terror* (Cambridge, Mass., 1935)
—— *The Incidence of the Emigration during the French revolution* (Cambridge, Mass., 1951)
PALMER, R. R., *Twelve who ruled* (Princeton, 1959) (Committee of Public Safety)
WILKINSON, S., *The French army before Napoleon* (Oxford, 1915)
BRINTON, C., *The Jacobins* (New York, 1930)
GASTON-MARTIN, *Les Jacobins* (1945)
MATHIEZ, A., *La vie chère et le mouvement social sous la Terreur* (1927)
ROSE, R. B., *The Enragés; Socialists of the French revolution?* (Melbourne, 1965)
DUBREUIL, L., *Histoire des insurrections de l'Ouest*, 2 vols. (1929–30)
GUERIN, D., *La lutte des classes sous la première république*, 2 vols. (Neo-Marxist) (1946)
BOULOISEAU, M., *Le comité de Salut Public*
JACOB, L., *Les suspects pendant la révolution, 1789–1794* (1952)
SOBOUL, A., *Les Sans-Culottes Parisiens en l'an II* (1958) (Available in English trans-lation central part only) *The Parisian Sans-Culottes in the French Revolution, 1793–1794*, trans. G. Lewis (Oxford, 1964)

Совв, R., *Les armées révolutionnaires. Instruments de la Terreur dans les Départements, Avril 1793—Floréal An. II*, 2 vols. (1961–3)
—— *Terreur et Subsistances, 1793–1795* (1965)

Chapter 10
MATHIEZ, A., *Robespierre Terroriste* (1921)
—— *Etudes Robespierristes*, 2 vols. (1917–18)
CAMILLE DESMOULINS, *Le Vieux Cordelier*, ed. H. Calvet (1936)
LEFEBVRE, G., *Questions agraires au temps de la Terreur* (Strasbourg, 1932)
ORDING, A., *Le bureau de police du comité de Salut Public* (Oslo, 1930)
LEFEBVRE, G., *Les Thermidoriens* (1957). English trans. by R. Baldick (London, 1965)
—— *Le Directoire* (1950) ——
Maximilien Robespierre, 1758–1794. Beiträge zu seinem 200 Geburtstag, ed. W. Markov (Berlin, 1958)
TØNNESSON, K. D., *La Défaite des Sans-Culottes; Mouvement Populaire et réaction bourgeoise en l'an III* (1959)

INDEX

hARpER ⚜ CORChBOOKS

American Studies: General

HENRY STEELE COMMAGER, Ed.: The Struggle for Racial Equality TB/1300

CARL N. DEGLER, Ed.: Pivotal Interpretations of American History TB/1240, TB/1241

A. S. EISENSTADT, Ed.: The Craft of American History: Recent Essays in American Historical Writing
Vol. I TB/1255; Vol. II TB/1256

CHARLOTTE P. GILMAN: Women and Economics ‡ TB/3073

MARCUS LEE HANSEN: The Immigrant in American History TB/1120

JOHN HIGHAM, Ed.: The Reconstruction of American History △ TB/1068

ROBERT H. JACKSON: The Supreme Court in the American System of Government TB/1106

LEONARD W. LEVY, Ed.: American Constitutional Law: Historical Essays TB/1285

LEONARD W. LEVY, Ed.: Judicial Review and the Supreme Court TB/1296

LEONARD W. LEVY: The Law of the Commonwealth and Chief Justice Shaw TB/1309

RALPH BARTON PERRY: Puritanism and Democracy TB/1138

ARNOLD ROSE: The Negro in America TB/3048

American Studies: Colonial

BERNARD BAILYN, Ed.: The Apologia of Robert Keayne: Self-Portrait of a Puritan Merchant TB/1201

BERNARD BAILYN: The New England Merchants in the Seventeenth Century TB/1149

JOSEPH CHARLES: The Origins of the American Party System TB/1049

CHARLES GIBSON: Spain in America † TB/3077

LAWRENCE HENRY GIPSON: The Coming of the Revolution: 1763-1775. † Illus. TB/3007

PERRY MILLER & T. H. JOHNSON, Eds.: The Puritans: A Sourcebook Vol. I TB/1093; Vol. II TB/1094

EDMUND S. MORGAN, Ed.: The Diary of Michael Wigglesworth, 1653-1657 TB/1228

EDMUND S. MORGAN: The Puritan Family TB/1227

RICHARD B. MORRIS: Government and Labor in Early America TB/1244

WALLACE NOTESTEIN: The English People on the Eve of Colonization: 1603-1630. † Illus. TB/3006

JOHN P. ROCHE: Origins of American Political Thought: Selected Readings TB/1301

JOHN SMITH: Captain John Smith's America: Selections from His Writings. Ed. with Intro. by John Lankford TB/3078

American Studies: From the Revolution to 1860

MAX BELOFF, Ed.: The Debate on the American Revolution, 1761-1783: A Sourcebook △ TB/1225

RAY A. BILLINGTON: The Far Western Frontier: 1830-1860. † Illus. TB/3012

EDMUND BURKE: On the American Revolution. ‡ Edited by Elliott Robert Barkan TB/3068

WHITNEY R. CROSS: The Burned-Over District TB/1242

GEORGE DANGERFIELD: The Awakening of American Nationalism: 1815-1828. † Illus. TB/3061

WILLIAM W. FREEHLING, Ed.: The Nullification Era: A Documentary Record ‡ TB/3079

FRANCIS GRIERSON: The Valley of Shadows: The Coming of the Civil War in Lincoln's Midwest TB/1246

JAMES MADISON: The Forging of American Federalism. Edited by Saul K. Padover TB/1226

JOHN C. MILLER: Alexander Hamilton and the Growth of the New Nation TB/3057

RICHARD B. MORRIS, Ed.: The Era of the American Revolution TB/1180

FRANCIS S. PHILBRICK: The Rise of the West, 1754-1830. † Illus. TB/3067

American Studies: Since the Civil War

W. R. BROCK: An American Crisis: Congress and Reconstruction, 1865-67 ° △ TB/1283

W. A. DUNNING: Reconstruction, Political and Economic: 1865-1877 TB/1073

ROBERT GREEN MCCLOSKEY: American Conservatism in the Age of Enterprise: 1865-1910 TB/1137

VERNON LANE WHARTON: The Negro in Mississippi: 1865-1890 TB/1178

A. RUSSELL BUCHANAN: The United States and World War II. † Illus. Vol. II TB/3044; Vol. II TB/3045

FOSTER RHEA DULLES: America's Rise to World Power: 1898-1954. † Illus. TB/3021

ROBERT L. HEILBRONER: The Limits of American Capitalism TB/1305

SIDNEY HOOK: Reason, Social Myths, and Democracy TB/1237

WILLIAM E. LEUCHTENBURG: Franklin D. Roosevelt and the New Deal: 1932-1940. † Illus. TB/3025

ARTHUR S. LINK: Woodrow Wilson and the Progressive Era: 1910-1917. † Illus. TB/3023

GEORGE E. MOWRY: The Era of Theodore Roosevelt and the Birth of Modern America: 1900-1912. † TB/3022

RUSSEL B. NYE: Midwestern Progressive Politics: 1870-1958 TB/1202

WILLIAM PRESTON, JR.: Aliens and Dissenters: Federal Suppression of Radicals, 1903-1933 TB/1287

JACOB RIIS: The Making of an American. ‡ Edited by Roy Lubove TB/3070

PHILIP SELZNICK: TVA and the Grass Roots: A Study in the Sociology of Formal Organization TB/1230

IDA M. TARBELL: The History of the Standard Oil Company: Briefer Version.‡ Edited by David M. Chalmers TB/3071

GEORGE B. TINDALL, Ed.: A Populist Reader ‡ TB/3069

---

† The New American Nation Series, edited by Henry Steele Commager and Richard B. Morris.

‡ American Perspectives series, edited by Bernard Wishy and William E. Leuchtenburg.

* The Rise of Modern Europe series, edited by William L. Langer.

** History of Europe series, edited by J. H. Plumb.

¶ Researches in the Social, Cultural, and Behavioral Sciences, edited by Benjamin Nelson.

§ The Library of Religion and Culture, edited by Benjamin Nelson.

Σ Harper Modern Science Series, edited by James R. Newman.

° Not for sale in Canada.

△ Not for sale in the U. K.

2

36-202